How Things Fit Together

The Katharine Bakeless Nason Literary Publication Prizes

The Bakeless Literary Publication Prizes are sponsored by the Bread Loaf Writers' Conference of Middlebury College to support the publication of first books. The manuscripts are selected through an open competition and are published by University Press of New England / Middlebury College Press.

1999 Competition Winners

Poetry

Jill Alexander Essbaum, *Heaven*
judge: Agha Shahid Ali

Fiction

Adria Bernardi, *The Day Laid on the Altar*
judge: Andrea Barrett

Nonfiction

Kevin Oderman, *How Things Fit Together*
judge: Scott Russell Sanders

How Things Fit Together

fifteen essays

Kevin Oderman

A Middlebury / Bread Loaf Book

Published by University Press of New England

Hanover & London

Middlebury College Press
Published by University Press of New England, Hanover, NH 03755
© 2000 by Kevin Oderman
All rights reserved
Printed in the United States of America
5 4 3 2 1

"Two Step on the Threshing Floor," "Balkan Walks," "The Living Daylights," "In the At-
tic of Memory," and "My Last Caribou" first appeared in the *Northwest Review*; "Kinds
of Motion" and "How Things Fit Together " appeared in the *Southwest Review*; "Fool's
Journey" and "Hunting on Human Ground" appeared in the *North American Review*;
"Dead Totems" appeared in *Flyway*; "Troglodyte Nights: In Cappadocia," "Dr.
Williams's Medicine Bundle," "A Coleridge Walk," and "Go Back On," appeared in the
North Dakota Quarterly; "Viburnum" is reprinted from *Shenandoah: The Washington
and Lee University Review*, with the permission of the editor.

Library of Congress Cataloging-in-Publication Data

Oderman, Kevin, 1951–
How things fit together : fifteen essays / Kevin Oderman
p.   cm. — (A Middlebury/Bread Loaf Book)
"The Katharine Bakeless Nason literary publication prizes."
ISBN 1–58465–047–8 (cloth : alk. paper)
I. Title. II. Series.
AC8.018   2000
081—dc 21   00–023145

For Ambrose and Virginia Oderman

TABLE OF CONTENTS

How Things Fit Together

How Things Fit Together

1. Morris Chair

I am thinking of James Agee's *A Death in the Family,* a dreamy kind of thinking, not trying to figure much out—just lying down close with my love for the book. It's a story about how a family, the Follets, is sundered by the death of the father, Jay. That breakage, not remembered because not forgotten, looms behind what I am remembering the way the gray clouds of a coming storm stand behind a tree or a bush, or a chair left in the yard that the last of the sun has picked out in the foreground and made to look loved. Half of what I'm doing is just marveling at how the book holds me, how I'm bound to it and have been for twenty years or more.

Now I'm thinking about how Jay's Morris chair is implicated in all this. The copy of the book I first read, a tan paperback, figured the chair on the cover and nothing else but the title and the author's name. Roughly drawn, the chair—a massive, wooden, slat-sided affair—is empty, but the light-colored cushions show the shape of the man who once sat there. That human impression on the cushions became, by the time I finished the book, Jay's shape. The chair bore Jay's mark, not only in its cushions but everywhere, the mark of his choosing it, using it. The bond between the man and the chair was something far more in-

Line drawings by Sylvia Torning.

timate and enduring than just owning it. The family, familiars of the house, knew this, and the sight of the empty chair in their midst unsettled them. Rufus, Jay's young son, knew too. "He looked at his father's morsechair. . . . With a sense of deep stealth and secrecy he finally went over and stood beside it. After a few moments, and after listening most intently, to be sure that nobody was near, he smelled of the chair, its deeply hollowed seat, the arms, the back." Far down in this, not articulated but palpably there, I understand something about how a house and the way it's furnished can register, can mean home. And I understand something about how Agee's work in English creates that Morris chair—a chair made of words—and makes it speak to me of home.

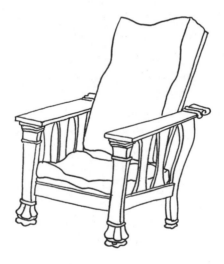

Once or twice in the years after I first read *A Death in the Family*, I happened on Morris chairs, big flat-armed things fitted out with a reclining back. I didn't yet know how to see them; for me, they came bound within the frame of Agee's chair and that was enough. I wanted one. The experience wasn't novel, for me anyway; hadn't I carried a Russian samovar bought in Athens all over Europe one student summer, and then

brought it home, in memory of those conversations around the
samovar in the novels of Dostoyevsky?

"Morsechair," little Rufus thought, addressing himself to his father's empty chair. A chair with a name. For Rufus, the name
had a purely domestic resonance; it was a synonym for his father's chair. But the Morris chair got its name from William
Morris, the English poet and a leading light in the English Arts
and Crafts movement. In revolt against what the industrial revo-
lution had done to home life, to family, and in revolt against the
shoddiness of factory-made goods, the Arts and Crafters sought
to reestablish a guild system so that people could live as artisans
and things be well made.

By the turn into the twentieth century, the Arts and Crafts
movement had begun to attract exponents on the west side of
the Atlantic as well. Soon they too were making furniture, including Morris chairs, and a range of solidly crafted things for
the home. The best known of the Arts and Crafts converts and
perhaps the most philosophical among them were Gustav Stickley, of the Craftsman Workshops, and Elbert Hubbard, of the
Roycroft Shops. They had their imitators, a lot of them. Many of
the imitators turned out real goods some of the time; a few, L. &
J. G. Stickley, Limbert, Stickley Brothers, and Lifetime, most of
the time. But many others did not. They made Arts and Crafts,
"Mission"-looking furniture, and more or less returned to the
level of shoddiness that had started the wheel turning in the first
place.

Reading catalog copy written by Gustav Stickley, Charles
Limbert, or Elbert Hubbard, I am struck by the degree to which
the structure of the furniture figured in how it was sold: how it fit
together and the promise that it would stay put together. The
idea of ornament was subsumed under the idea of structure and
materials; the grain of the wood and the details of its construction were themselves thought to provide sufficient ornament.

❀ ❀ ❀

I like to think, and have come to imagine, that Jay's "morsechair" was one of those well-made chairs, say from the shop of L. & J. G. Stickley near Syracuse. The dates are right. A chair brought home early in the century would have had time to respond to Jay's shape, to have a little of a man's smell, by the time of his death in 1915. The Arts and Crafts movement in America went into decline that same year: Gustav Stickley closed the Craftsman Workshops, and Elbert Hubbard went to the bottom in the *Lusitania*.

Mortise and Tenon

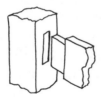 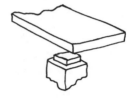

A Mission chair's being well made depended on the joiner's art. The art wasn't new or news; most of its operations were traditional, with origins so old they were no longer inquired of. The root problem, simply put, was how to fit the pieces together, how to overcome the separateness of the parts in favor of the integrity of the whole: joinery. The idea admits of metaphorical extension, surely: how words fit together, shoddily or well, how people stay together or don't. At some point I came to understand that the attraction of a thing well-made is itself *made,* of the thing and these metaphors, that they are all joined together against the fast slide in time to dissolution.

Jay's Morris chair, if it was any good at all, would have been constructed with mortise-and-tenon joints. The mortises, rectangular pockets cut into the posts, would have received the tenons of the stretchers coming across. The posts themselves would have been cut down into tenons at the top to join a mortise chiseled into the arms, which lay across the posts. The skirts and stretchers would have been wide, wide enough to support big mortise-and-tenon joints and the large glue surfaces such construction makes possible.

But to make a joint secure, for use, the best of the Mission craftsmen did not depend on glue alone. They pegged the joint —first boring a hole through the mortise and on into the tenon, then driving a wooden peg into the hole. A single peg secured the post to the arms—maybe two, top and bottom, for the skirt in front and for the stretchers. Such joints are tough; I've hardly ever seen one that's given way. Breakage is possible; but if it happens, it's the strength of the wood as much as the strength of the joint that's in question.

Arts and Crafts furniture makers advertised pegged mortise-and-tenon joints in the introductions to their catalogs and, in the catalog drawings, often indicated where the pegs were with small circles. The furniture itself featured them; the pegs were sometimes left a little raised or stained a little darker, the peg taking the color of fuming or dyeing more. It wasn't long after I began to take an interest in Mission furniture that my eyes learned to look first for pegged joints. They were the strength of the furniture and also a sign of that strength. I'd seen plenty of poorly constructed furniture gone to pieces, every chair and cabinet a reminder of the general dissolution all things suffer, that we suffer. The craft of things built to last provides a kind of solace for our losses, a limited warranty: even if it's all going in the end, it doesn't have to go before the end.

Through-Tenon

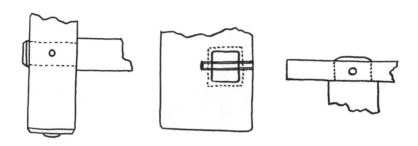

Etymologically, the strength of mortise-and-tenon construction lies in the tenon, a word that means, at root, "to hold." Tenons hold. But where they hold is invisible: the joint is inside. There might be something else hidden inside (a dowel joint, for instance, so often the culprit in furniture gone to pieces). Pegs promise mortise-and-tenon construction but can be quite unobtrusive; through-tenons are not. Often, Arts and Crafts furniture has mortises cut clear through; the tenon is fitted to extend beyond the surface of the joined piece. In chairs this would most often be seen on the arms, with the posts' tenons pushing through, but sometimes stretchers too have tenons extending through the posts. The real joinery remains out of sight, in the dark of the matter, but through-tenons make the construction more visible and provide, as the craftsmen said, "structural ornament." The term contrasts—or was meant to—with "applied ornament" or, more generally, with any ornamentation other than the beauty of the materials and how they're put together.

It's a sad irony that through-tenons were soon "applied" by furniture makers satisfied with the *look* of structure. Bits of wood fashioned to ape through-tenons were stuck on wherever they looked good—on a post opposite stretchers or on the arms above the posts. Structure, in these pieces, succumbed to fashion.

Tenon and Key

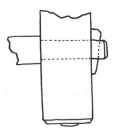

More often on tables and cabinets than on chairs, but occasionally on chairs, the tenons extended through and then some, leaving wood enough for a mortise to be chiseled through the tenon, into which a "key" was tapped home, locking the pieces together. This provided additional structural ornament and, although the actual joint remained inside, featured the joinery even more clearly than through-tenons.

If my love for Arts and Crafts furniture began with reading Agee's *A Death in the Family,* the "key" that held me, holds me, is mortality itself, and how that promise conditions how I think about what I want around me while I live. I do not want my own time here to seem long against a background of disposable goods, things that go to the dump before I go to the grave. Maybe it's possible to make life seem longer than it is by outliving the things around you, but it's a false promise. I am the transient here; we are all, like Jay, soon to leave empty chairs. For now, I want to sit down in chairs that outlasted the people who sat in them first, that will outlast me too. That such chairs are old is part of what calls to me, but that they have lasted because of how the pieces were joined is most of the rest of it. I want an art longer than lifetimes. I want a life grounded in such art.

❀ ❀ ❀

When I look at the drawing of Jay's Morris chair on the cover of
A Death in the Family now, I think it's a pretty sad piece of work.
The front posts are square and massive but terminate in something fluted, perhaps even in a claw foot. The rear posts bow out
like the legs of a tired horse. The chair has a facade: it is more
massive up front, where the size of the legs is built up with applied ridges. The chair pretends. There are no pegged joints to
suggest mortise-and-tenon construction and certainly no
through-tenons. It doesn't look like a chair meant to last.

I'm thinking the artist got it wrong. By the fifties, when the
book was published, the Arts and Crafts movement was in
eclipse. Agee himself died before the work was quite completed
and so was not there to object. His book, so well made its finish-
ing could be left to editors, persists. I realize now it was the language of the book that initially charged my response to the
cover, that led me to know something, to ask hard questions before I invite any chair, any thing, into my house. I wouldn't invite
the artist's misbegotten Morris chair, that recliner, in. I don't
think the Follets would have either. I'm thinking they'd have
preferred a big, Onondaga Shops L. & J. G. Stickley Morris
chair: massive posts at all four corners with tenons extending
through the broad, flat arms. The skirt, front and back, is joined
to the posts with double-pegged through-tenons. The stretchers, running near the ground, are also joined to the posts with
pegged through-tenons. There are five wide slats climbing up
from each of the stretchers into the arms, giving the chair a
closed feel. The wide arms are supported with corbels on all
four posts. The back adjusts, a wood cross-piece fitting into
notches cut into the arms behind the ladder back. The chair
has deep leather cushions, stitched boldly with thongs, cushions that show a man's shape, Jay's shape. The oak has been
fumed and glows through a dusky wax finish. All the chair's
beauty is in its proportions, in the wood and the leather and

how the pieces fit together. Nothing lasts forever, but that chair was meant to last a long time.

2. Somno

We call most of the rooms of our houses after what we do in them—dining room, living room, study. Not the bedroom. It's called after the bed, furniture. Perhaps this is because no room is so dominated by a single piece of furniture as the bedroom. The bed is where we sleep and hope most to join ourselves in love. When I think about what a bed is, I find it hard not to remember the scene near the end of Homer's *Odyssey*, the one where Penelope tries Odysseus by suggesting their bed be hauled out of the bedroom. He'd been away for a long time, so long he was no longer recognizable as the man who'd sailed out for Troy. Penelope, to be sure of her man, suggests moving the bed, because only the two of them know that it cannot be moved, that one of the bedposts was hewn from an olive tree that still has its roots in the ground. So when Odysseus speaks again, Penelope knows for sure, at last, who speaks to her, knows that a marriage thought broken is restored.

Odysseus, in his response, emphasizes how he'd made the

bed from a young olive tree, how it was constructed. He reminds her how he'd pruned away the leaves and branches and, starting from the ground, shaped the trunk into a bedpost with a bronze adze, bored holes through it with an auger. He reminds her how he'd fashioned three more posts to match, built a frame, and stretched a web of oxhide thongs across that frame, to make the bed.

The pieces were joined together and joined to the earth; on that bed, Odysseus joined with Penelope to create again, Telemachus. And Homer built it all in words, constructed the story well enough to endure centuries of oral transmission and endless translation and retelling, as I'm doing here, encouraging that olive tree to show the silver and green of its leaves yet again.

Tongue and Groove

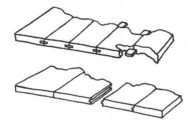

But I digress. A bed may dominate the bedroom, but I was thinking about a nightstand, sometimes called a "somno" in books about Arts and Crafts furniture. The name is a bit pretentious, but I like it for suggesting that the thing attends me while I'm dozing. It's for setting a book on, when I trade the dream of story for the glistening screen of sleep. The bedroom is all threshold, where we leave this world for another. Perhaps we furnish it for how we live in it awake, but I don't think only for that. We leave more lightly, in sleep and in death, knowing what we leave behind is as we wanted it.

So I've been looking for a Mission somno, or perhaps a cellarette to use as a somno, to sit next to my bed. I've learned to wait, maybe a long time, for the right thing, learned long ago that having nothing is better than having the wrong thing.

A somno—any kind of cabinet—requires fitting planks together to make the top and sides. Sometimes tops are simply glued, side to side, but such a joint is weak and often splits with use or weather. It's a problem that admits of different solutions. Some Mission workshops, notably L. & J. G. Stickley's, used a spline. Narrow rips were cut into the sides of the planks, and the spline, a thin strip of wood, was glued into the notch. Most other workshops made use of tongue-and-groove joinery. A square protrusion, the tongue, was cut out of one side of the plank, a matching groove into the other. The planks were then fit together, a tongue in every groove.

It's hard to know what the joiner had in mind when he made the name "tongue and groove." But some things in language hold, and the words stay together, names, idioms, poems. They don't last forever, but the strongest of them lasts longer than the tongue and lips that first formed them. We speak such things every day, the mystery of their joinery hidden from us.

Butterfly

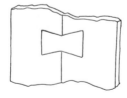

The sides of a somno, or cellarette, might be formed of planks joined tongue and groove, or perhaps chamfered (the edges of the planks cut at a forty-five-degree angle). Occasionally, the boards in a door were joined with "butterflies," wood tenons shaped like a bow tie and inserted into corresponding mortises

in the boards, one wing on each of the joined boards. The butterflies were left a little raised and were so ornamental they were
countenanced only because of their function.

A more recent paperback edition of James Agee's *A Death in
the Family* has a cover that no longer features Jay's Morris chair
but instead shows the bereaved family, his wife, daughter, and
little Rufus, surrounded by the wings of a butterfly, Psyche. That
butterfly figures in the story at the funeral. It landed on Jay's
coffin, over his heart, and stayed there, pulsing, as the coffin was
lowered into the grave, "all the way down."

Dovetail

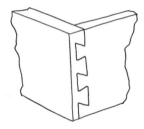

If there's a drawer, the front will be joined to the rails by means
of dovetails, a row of fan-shaped tenons cut into the end of the
rail and fitted snugly into a row of corresponding mortises in the
side of the drawer front. Of course, the joiner who said "dove-
tail" could have said any bird, or something else entirely. But the
name held. Birds and butterflies in the joinery lighten the
weight of Mission furniture—not its weight on the scale, which
should be heavy, but the weight of how it rests in the mind. And
how odd that the butterfly, pagan Psyche, and the dove, the
Church's spirit, should have found their way into the wood, into
how it's joined.

So I'm looking for something to go next to my bed where
there's nothing now—a cabinet, something with a little darkness
closed behind a small door. I'll keep a few things in there. A

magic stone from Hathor's precincts at Dendera. A hand ax out of the Sahara. A thumb ring from submerged Nubia, for casting out devils. A flask of Heaven Hill.

I'm looking for a somno made at the Craftsman Workshops by Gustav Stickley around 1901. It has a flat top and an open shelf below, both tongue-and-groove. Under the shelf, there is a closed cabinet, which hangs a few inches off the floor. The square cabinet door is built of five pieces, the middle piece square, too, and recessed. It looks a little like a safe but has no key; it is closed only by a pyramidal wooden knob. Through-tenons run under the shelf and the bottom of the cabinet, pinned through the sides of the thick posts.

Or I'm looking for a cellarette from the Onandaga Shops, made by L. & J. G. Stickley around 1905. It has a splined plank top and is closed almost to the ground. The corners are constructed from chamfered boards built on an internal frame. They are connected, on all sides, by arched skirts. There is a drawer, just under the top, where the doves are, and the three boards of the door are joined by four butterflies. There is a key, for locking spirits away. The cabinet has an owlish look.

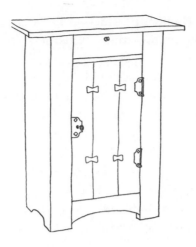

Even while I'm looking, I know what I find will likely be something else altogether.

3. Fire

Gustav Stickley's shopmark, a joiner's compass, bore the Flemish legend *Als ik Kan* (as I can), that is, as best I can. It promised workmanship, the structure of well-made furniture. They were the only words that went out of the shop *on* the furniture, but they called up the whole Arts and Crafts aesthetic, the language the furniture was wrapped in, which as much as the furniture itself was what bound people to it. Still is.

Almost everything comes wrapped in words, of course. Sometimes it seems that the words get most of the attention, and what they're wrapped around little enough. And when things come unglued, we shudder to see what we've been sold. It happens all the time. Not just with furniture. It's not that we need to attend to language less and things more. We need to attend more, be more like Rufus inching up on his father's "morsechair," whether it's words or the world we're sniffing, to taste, as Agee said, "the mean goodness" of our living. It's what we can do.

I remember once, in Santa Barbara, hearing a woman from up in the hills, from Montecito, indignantly exclaiming over houseguests from a long-ago winter. She'd left a key for acquaintances up from Los Angeles, being away herself. "Those people broke up our old Mission furniture with hammers," she said, "and burned it in the fireplace, for heat, or just to hear it crackle." You can make a home to last and still find, at the end, disaster. Maybe it's the common lot. Some fires burn slowly, is all.

Viburnum: On Moving On

Whenever I pack my books—it seems often—I recall a legend I read many moves ago in one of them, perhaps in Helen Waddell's *Desert Fathers* or maybe in one of the volumes of A. J. Festugiere's *Les Moines d'Orient*. I'd check the reference for you, but that shelf is packed, and it's legend, after all, the stuff of retelling. One of the holy anchorites had died in a rocky place, and the job of removing him had been undertaken by another monk and a donkey. When it was time to load up, the holy dead father was lashed on one side of the donkey, his worldly possessions, his "books," on the other, and *the balance was perfect*.

It's a wonderful image, weighed in the balance and found just, and cautionary. But I can never hold it for long in my mind before another image unseats it. I imagine my own rotund self strapped on one side of a donkey, my books on the other, and then it happens: either the donkey collapses in an ignominious heap or the pallet of books slams down, and I, with considerable loss of dignity, catapult over the donkey's back, a new moon over the *scetes*.

I don't often think of the desert fathers between moves, almost never. There is little in the settled life of the professor that calls to them. But I lived a season under their spell, and a good stain remains that I find again when I box my books. Books are heavy; they make me feel heavy. Moving reminds me of the weight of possessions, what having them says about me.

Of course, the dead anchorite of this legend was not being praised for having so few books, not by the standards of the *scetes*. The advice there was to sell your books to the last one, even *the* book, and to distribute the proceeds to the poor. No, the legend intimates a way of life and a final accord.

There is little mere about the association that calls this legend up come moving time. There's more to it than a book in the hand. Contrary to the popular recital, we do not move into the future when we move from one place to another. We move into the past, our past. It wells up, forming and re-forming, until we're well settled, when it dies down again. Every move contains a reckoning, not a final balance but a provisional accounting. It doesn't require figuring; the sums float up. Nor can any reckoning remain personal, though it may seem that way; the worlds we live in are as much in us as we are in them.

To realize, then, that I move into the past when I move witnesses against the fraudulent metaphors we live by. And under the metaphor that teaches us that we move into the future— supporting it, trance-deep and invisible—lies our metaphorical relation to time, that the future is *in front of us*, the past *behind*. We are turned, bodily, toward the future; it's difficult to imagine another way and just as difficult to realize how far-reaching the implications of this stance might be. It all came home to me one evening while I was reading a learned note in W. B. Stanford's commentary on the *Odyssey*—my head snapped back as if I had just sniffed an ampule of smelling salts: The ancient "Greeks regarded the past as what lay before them (πρόσσω), the future as what lay behind (ὀπίσσω), i.e., their mental orientation was towards the known." The mind reels at what this suggests about us.

How things get turned around! And upside down: even an inconspicuous word like *sums*, the provisional sums of moving mentioned above, has turned in time. Sums is from *summus*, the

highest thing (summit), because Greeks and Romans added
from the bottom up and wrote their totals at the top. We add
down, and write our "sums" on the "bottom line."

Packing up poses dangers for a bad back. Last time I move, mine
sprang when I carelessly lifted a potted plant, a pot of earth. If
my spine had been an exclamation, that day it bent to a question.
The staff I'd found in a dim corner of the basement when we
moved in at last found a use; I bent over it, suddenly old—one
eye stretched wide, the other drawn down into a narrow squint.

That last night there I slept on the floor, an agony, and
dreamed: We were driving a rocky desert in watery light; I
thought, "at the extreme edge of civilization." The small track
gave out. I pulled the car into a gully to turn around, got out, and
spotted a curious little toad with one big eye in the middle of its
forehead. I watched, dumb, as a bird's head poked through the
eye; then the whole toad stretched, and it was a shore bird, stiffly
walking, pecking at the sand, and when it pecked, a claw—crab
or lobster—extended from its mouth to the ground, then retracted, then extended and retracted. Such is the loose change
of moving.

Here, we unpacked at the edge of the city, our windows
turned away, on fields, empty lots dreaming of prairie. Someone
had stuck a little tree in the ground twenty yards out from the
dining room window; it had not taken, a tangle of leafless twigs.
Still, the birds came to it. Soon after arriving I saw a tanager
there that, true to its name (walk about), had wandered from its
home ground.

That dead tree, carelessly transplanted, can be exactly said to
have "failed to put down roots." However, while such a literal
use of the phrase "to put down roots" may charm with its horti-
cultural precision, it's an infrequent usage. In roots, metaphor
rules. Those who move are uprooted, or worse, rootless. It's a
metaphor favored by those who stay on, who belong. It flatters

them their staying put as "having roots." But even for those who stay, the metaphor has ambiguous implications. At best, it favors place, favors stewards. And it holds the local against the homogenizing "out there." Still, it's xenophobic, excluding. Curiously, those who move, the rootless of this metaphor, espouse it as well, forever saying, as newcomers, how much they look forward to putting down roots. It's expected. It voices the wanderer's submission to the mores of the new place.

We hadn't been in our new place nine months (full term, or two semesters for the professor) when whoever owned the little tree, whoever it was who had stuck it there to begin with, changed his mind in favor of a duplex on that spot. The man's bulldozer upended it, left it upside down, sticking, a little obliquely, from the side of a new hill. Perhaps it's a sorry commentary on how the tree looked right side up, but its appearance was not greatly changed by its new purchase on the earth. I was surprised and heartened to discover birds perching in the little tree's roots that first evening. Later, of course, the bulldozer reduced it to sticks. But the image remained: the upended tree, with its roots not in terra firma but in firmament. It grew in me.

It's a curious thing how connections get made, how even a bulldozer has a place in mental excavations. Seeing the metaphor of roots stood on its head helped me to realize how pedestrian it is, how it defines us by our feet. It casts us not as Saunterers, the sovereign Holy-Landers of Thoreau's "Walking," but as vegetable and fixed, with roots going down through our soles into the earth to suck up sustenance. Chthonic, we sup in the underworld. And so we are called *human*, after our father who art in *humus*. By this account we are earthlings indeed.

A clayey materiality sticks to all this. But as my little tree reminds me, there are other versions of this story. From the Upanishads to the Zohar to Dante, the tree of life grows down, its roots drinking in sun and blue heaven. Perhaps this is a more sustaining story for nomads who live by moving on.

Some of this may have been already playing on my consciousness when I bought the nomad's rug my feet now rest on. We never had such rugs when I was growing up: I knew them only in books—and there only as magic carpets. Having one meant one thing to me: joining the birds, no longer earthbound. Of course, the magic doesn't work for adults; and far from carrying me, I carry *it* whenever I move. But it is portable, and where I roll it out I feel at home. At first I thought it was the rug's color that spoke to me, the night-sky blue ground and somber reds. It took some time for what the rug said to break through my ignorance (the iconographical impulse was somewhat dilute in the suburbs of my childhood). Still, one day I stopped thinking of design and saw, within the elongated central hexagon, the tree of life that had been growing there from the beginning. With a little digging in the library, I was soon able to discover three stylized birds in that tree, which seemed to be in flower with stars of Solomon. Looking at it now, I see it more clearly. The magical stars don't hang like blossoms from the tree's limbs but are tangled in its roots, which sprout at both ends on the rug's night-blue field. Viewed from either end, this tree hangs down, from a night sky that is always there. Even flat on the floor it's a rug that floats in air.

I recognize in all this a predilection for the upside-down view of things. To a degree, this is probably quirk. I suppose I was born head down, which would explain everything. I don't remember moves that far back. I do remember, however, the first time I consciously took the upside down view of things. I was an adolescent and not good with girls, though I had a girlfriend I visited often. I knew the times called on me to be "cool" on these visits, but I could rarely manage it. One afternoon, over there, the thing hit me. Without pause I dropped to the ground and rolled into a wobbly headstand, announcing to my dazed girlfriend that I had that Atlas guy figured out: you didn't have to be a strong man to hold the world up; all you needed was balance. She was a tolerant girl, perhaps not wholly cool herself; in the end she consented to join me, and there we stood, upside down on the front lawn, reflecting on the view.

The Atlas of my childhood was image only: a strong man with bent knees bearing the globe high on his shoulders. I'm not sure where that image came from, perhaps from the side of an Atlas Van Lines truck (in the beginning was the logo). But all through childhood I knew Atlas only in this posture, as a man displaying his strength in titanic feat. I didn't know then that the earth-bearing Atlas of Atlas Van Lines (who is a furniture mover, after all, but bigger, whose burden is a world of possessions) was not the Atlas of myth at all; that Atlas bore the heavens on the palms of his hands. It's a curious reversal but now largely complete. Our Atlas is the world bearer.

You, reader, may be expecting me to claim that when I move from one place to another I trust my books and rugs to Atlas, but no. I drive myself (auto-mobile). I do consult a road atlas on occasion. That atlas gets its name from early map books, which bore the figure of the heaven-bearing Atlas of myth on their frontispiece, though the world-bearing Atlas would have been more appropriate, and even then an atlas carries rather less than a world in carrying maps of the world.

If I had hired a mover, I might never have lifted the potted fig nor sprung my back. But I did, and when I went to have its question answered, I discovered a map of the spine in the waiting room. And there, at the top and supporting the head, I found it: the atlas vertebra. What *is* in a name? Is it the weight of a world we carry in our heads or weightless starry heavens?

Changes begin at the margins, at the margins of place, of consciousness, at the edge of a page. Moved in, I began again with

Emerson and Thoreau. I was not far into them before I found what I had taken to be the eccentric preoccupations of my own move in the public domain. The worlds we live in are as much in us as we are in them. As an antidote to the blindness of familiarity, Emerson exhorts, "Turn the eyes upside down, by looking at the landscape through your legs." Any front lawn is a good place to try. What's more, imagining Emerson making the discovery will defamiliarize him, too. And Emerson must have been troubled by the chthonic suggestions of the metaphor of roots, for he redacts with approbation the passage in Plato's *Timaeus* that "affirms a man to be a heavenly tree, growing with his root, which is his head, upward." Perhaps this is the true, radical man.

Thoreau's *Walden* (had I never noticed or forgotten?) is laced with ambiguity about which is the up and which the down side of things. The pond itself is a "lower heaven," "sky water." Thoreau too inverts his head, over the lake, to see its surface dematerialized, as "a thread of finest gossamer stretched across the valley." Fishing, Henry seems always in danger of casting his weight amid stars. Once, paddling on the lake over a school of perch, he found himself "in such transparent and seemingly bottomless water, reflecting the clouds, I seemed to be floating through the air as in a balloon, and their [the perch's] swimming impressed me as a kind of flight or hovering, as if they were a compact flock of birds passing beneath my level." Reading such stuff is disorienting, was probably meant to be, and implicitly calls into question what we think of as right side up, which supports subliminally Thoreau's overturning of the dominant cultural myths of his day (and ours).

Thoreau also has his tree. He proposes to rename White Pond "Yellow Pine Lake," because of a story he has unearthed about it. The broken trunk of a yellow pine had for years been seen projecting through the surface of the lake out in deep water. It was an oddity, and the locals presumed that the ground the pine stood on must have slumped, flooding what had been forest. Thoreau, in his precise way, documented the story at the

Massachusetts Historical Society, then found his own source at the lake. Indeed, Thoreau found the very man who had gotten the tree out over a decade before. He had done it in winter, sawing through the ice and dragging the tree out with oxen. But "before he had gone far in his work, he was surprised to find that it was wrong end upward, with the stumps of the branches pointing down, and the small end firmly fastened in the sandy bottom." Thoreau just tells this story; he doesn't read nature out loud here as he does so often in *Walden*. But I read Thoreau, and I know this tree. What does it say that for decades an upside-down tree was thought by the locals to be turned the other way around? What does it say that the roots, which should reach into sky, are broken off and that, in the end, the tree was removed with an eye to profit, the bottom line, but found good only for firewood, if for that?

Still, in the next paragraph it is clear that the possibility of the upside-down view of things was not pulled out with the tree: it's still there at the lake, in reflection (on reflection?): "the blue flag (*iris versicolor*) grows thinly in pure water, rising from the stony bottom all around the shore, where it is visited by hummingbirds in June; and the color both of its bluish blades and its flowers and especially their reflections, is in singular harmony with the glaucous water."

I remember the small orchard my father planted at the house where I grew up. Those trees took; in memory it is always harvest time, and my family has gathered to pick the blushing peaches and apricots. We had apple trees too, some of which bore four or five different varieties of apples. This was magic to me, even though I had seen my father bind the grafts with tar and strips cut from old inner tubes. The grafts not only lived, wonder enough, they bore fruit, which seemed to me even then to have the force of parable. I did not know as a boy that the word *graft* is from the Latin *graphium* (pencil) because a graft looks like a pencil, nor that further back yet the word is derived from the Greek *graphein* (to write). I like this etymology, for writing can graft shoot to tree, the personal to the public. Thoreau, of course, could fashion a pencil with his own hands and, having made it, knew what to do with it.

I am no Atlas nor want to be, but I do not want what strength I have dissipated by an unconscious struggle with the judgments embedded in the dominant metaphors of our language: uprooted, rootless. Who stays needs stories to stay well, who goes, stories to go well. A wanderer need not be a destroyer, nor does the mere act of staying make a steward. I read the other day that the Chinese ideogram for the Tao (the way) is composed of the character for a head over the character for the road. That might make a good story. One time, hiking a desert arroyo, I discovered in an eroded and dry creek bed juniper after juniper that clutched each its own ball of earth in its exposed roots, and they lived, witnesses. That too might make a good story. And perhaps it would be a good thing for the cosmopolitan to know that the zenith was not always a fixed point, that at root the word means the road overhead. *There* is a highway for moving on.

The Living Daylights

1.

Forget not yet
—Thomas Wyatt

Do I remember it? Or is it the story—real as any memory of what happened—that rides the water at the edge of forgetting? The river of memory and the river of forgetting run altogether, and the river of forgetting is the main stem.

Wrong Shoes

Wavering like a reflection on gliding water, I remember the bluff woman in front of the grocery cart, blocking our happy sailing through the aisles of the Safeway, asking the question, "Lady, you know your kid's got his shoes on the wrong feet?" I pulled back into the folds of my mother's skirt, a dark green curtain, a green field spotted with small, intensely pink flowers. I didn't hear my mother's answer, but the woman slipped behind us, and we were skimming again soon enough. I have no older memory, or I imagine nothing behind that encounter in the Safeway. The story begins there.

I was born bent-footed, and after a babyhood of casts, the

doctor had graduated me to wrong shoes for treatment. I walked into the world wearing them, a clownish little man, a figure of fun sometimes, but enjoying the general radiance of the sun. I was a small mote of consciousness in illumined liquid suspended over a pair of feet apparently heading two different directions.

Masked Men

Last year, on a sunny day, I visited the Portland Art Museum. Although I once had lived on the Park Blocks and visited the museum often, it was the first time I'd been back in years. I wanted to see again the collection of Native American things, see again something of the indigenous art of the Northwest, of the country I grew up in and still call home.

It was the Haida hats and cedar masks that I was drawn to. As always in museums, my pace was uneven. I walk by, unmoved and hardly looking, but then I am transfixed, unmoving, an obstruction to be negotiated by the museum-goers in "the traffic flow." I am indecorous, lost, apt to get down on my knees and press my nose against the glass.

I was absorbed by the masks within masks, hinged animal heads that swing open like double doors to reveal not a face but another mask. One, I remember, had the head of a raven, which opened to reveal the face of a man. They are called transformation masks. They remind me how things change, how identity can shift. Such masks are not for hiding behind.

Stopping before a bird-headed headdress, a Kwakiutl raven mask from Alert Bay, I was taken with the startling variety of its aspects, the way it changed as I shifted around its glass cabinet. Close, imagining wearing it, I received a shock, electrical; it wasn't the clumsy scrape of carved cedar or looking out of chinks I had imagined. No, I was a bird-headed man, when my head swung a black beak turned on the axis of my vision.

❊ ❊ ❊

Intending an Accident

A story was told about a dead boy, battered by traffic on a busy road. Some children ran breathless the quarter mile down the cross street, arms and legs flying, hysterical with news of the dead boy up on Glisan, knocked shapeless and bloody and dead. I was that boy. The kids said it was me, knew to tell Pearl, who was looking after me while my mother was away. Then they all rushed back up our street; Pearl must have looked large among those wild kids. What was on her face, in her burdened heart, expecting to find a dead boy when she had finished running? And where was I when she came in sight of the twisted shape on the road's shoulder, when the strength that was hers carried her close enough to discover it wasn't a boy, not me, but a clever dummy, daubed with red paint, not a dead boy?

I would have been asleep, dreaming in the woods perhaps or out back of Pearl's place, lost in looking at the owls that nested there. I didn't know I had been killed in effigy, thrown into traffic by rough boys at the other end of the block. When I wandered in, the story was over, had happened without me.

I never heard why the Darnell brothers chose my name for their dummy; I hardly knew them, can't remember anything about them now other than the malice of their prank, their desire to terrify. And yet, I knew them in their actions, even then, came to a dark suspicion, something about malevolence, some boys to be avoided, something in all of us better avoided.

I think now that I made my own dummy later on, or perhaps already had even then, someone called Kevin to sit in rooms where there was no air to breathe, while the live boy escaped through windows into the woods, into weedy but open fields. The bored boy, who could never subscribe, never see the point—that was the dummy, who only grimaced when called a sawdust head, sent to the ground again by men happy to watch an automaton doing push-ups. But if I abandoned the cardboard figure to his difficulties, the shadow that slunk off or an absence in the mannikin left behind, something there was provoking, called up malevolence. Or perhaps it was just the lack of faith, incredulity in the face of what passed for the world, just that which was provoking, calling into doubt what could only be supported by the rawest assertion. Perhaps that's why the battered dummy up on Glisan was a Kevin.

Fights

I didn't know as a kid, coming out of the woods, heading for home, for warmth, that the light of Oregon's Willamette Valley has a soft, muffled quality. It's wet, gray and white on foggy days, a gauzy bronze in the sun, especially in autumn, when the light rains over the yellow stubble. It was one of those days, the bronze light just giving way to the mother-of-pearl light of evening. I broke away from the woods and started across the open fields, felt the cool of evening begin to pull around my ankles.

When I heard my name called, I waved, absently, over my shoulder, bending in my mind toward home. Then I heard more calling and, looking back, saw another boy, Tommy, my age but small, chasing after me. I turned in time to see the belligerence in his face, to hear the challenge in his voice. He wanted to fight. There was no why about it. He came in swinging. I pushed him away, wary, using my reach, but the coolness of evening was in my veins, heat for fighting just wouldn't come. I fended him off, but he kept swinging, his small white fists flailing. Finally, heart cold in my chest, I swung back, bloodied his nose, knocked him down. He swore and spit, got back up and charged. I hit him again, one sad thud after another. I pinned him down, pleading with him to give it up, crying myself, not wanting this, any of it, just wanting to get home out of the rising cold. This went on a long time. He wouldn't quit.

It was almost dark when Gary showed up. Older, bigger, he

tossed me off, his fists flashing up. What was I doing picking on Tommy? I laughed. A big kid picking on a little kid. Talking was out of the question. Gary hit me, and I laughed again. Soon enough I was laughing and crying both together. It hurt, the sting of the ache of a beating, but the pointlessness of it all, that's what appalled me. Those two boys going off together, hooting in the night, what did it all mean to them?

Best Friends

In the green world of springtime, grass again growing, the rush of sap in the trees, we children freed of our desks, pouring from the schoolroom door, out the long halls into the light. Then running in waves down the schoolyard hill, fanning out for home. One day, at the foot of the hill, there was a dog fight. The dogs had come to school to meet their young friends, but that day two of them fell to fighting, and when the kids spilled down the hill they found them, not posturing but fighting in dead earnest. The schoolboys and girls gathered in a ring around those two dogs, enthralled, their eyes fixed on the frothing, bloody dogs, their mouths hanging open. The dogs circled, tumbled, spit and blood matted, a guttural growling as they lunged to get their teeth on the jugular. Two small kids, crying, tried desperately to drag their dogs apart, but the dogs were all fear and rage, intent on a kill. At last a teacher waded through the crowd of children to kick the dogs apart, his own brutality written in every gesture, shouting at the children to get on home. The kids shuffled away, a little dashed, uneasy, knowing that they had wanted the fight to go on, that they too had wanted a killing. They were bewildered, at the last moment, at not having it. I remember a little girl, left behind, hanging on her dog, blood soaking her checked dress, her body heaving with strangled sobs. Maybe many in the crowd felt as I did, an icy paralysis suffusing the limbs, moved but unmoving, incapable of breaking from the spellbound ring.

Dropping Out

At kindergarten we were expected to be good boys and girls, to behave, but even misbehaving was a formal thing. It was a becoming, what had been animate became animated. Of course, the children were animated, a whirl of energy, a great din. But something had gone out of them, they were more like puppets than puppies. They made me uneasy, all those behaving and misbehaving boys and girls. But I wouldn't have fled if there hadn't been a wedge, something unbearable. It was a kiss. On birthdays, week after week, I saw the birthday boy or girl, smug on a chair, sitting on a table, a little throne, wearing a party hat. Then, after the singing, our teacher would lean over and kiss the child on the cheek. That, I knew it, was not going to happen to me. I walked home resolved: I wasn't going back. I wasn't made to.

When I had had enough of Sunday school—it didn't take long—I was allowed to drop out there too. I went to sit in a pew with my parents and brothers for the service upstairs. It was my first exposure to eloquence and to gleaming faith. The pastor rose, at times, into rapture, his glistening face radiant, suffused in benevolence. Looking around, I saw the heads of the fathers nodding on the edge of sleep, heard the stifled yawns, saw their furtiveness, adults pretending to pay attention. Afterward, as the congregation filed out the church doors, every gesture seemed feigned, a gesture forced on rigor.

My mother told me once—we were talking about children, what they know, when they come to consciousness—that one time when I was very little she found me in an empty room, kicking and punching the still air. "What on earth are you doing?" She asked. "Kicking God," I said. Kicking God! I remember my horror at the thought that everything could be, should be, known, that there was no hiding what was thought, what was done, from God. Now I am frightened, to trembling, that so little *can be* disclosed.

2.

> *It loved to happen*
> —Marcus Aurelius

In the evening, after I have finished up for the day, sometimes I sit by the ashes of the fire and whisper over the embers, see the light return to them, like memory. Long after the coals seem to have dissolved in ash, a little whisper is all it takes; there is still heat there, light. Then just a few dry shavings will bring the fire back.

Getting Education

The moment that I remember most fondly from all my years in schoolrooms, which still sustains me and guides me in my own teaching more than any other, took place in an anthropology seminar at Reed College. Something had been said, I hadn't heard what. I was away, in a half-dreaming, half-thinking state, the state in which things take shape. I was gone, and the professor, Gail Kelly, must have seen it; she called on me, just as many teachers had called on me during the years I had dreamed away in classrooms. "Mr. Oderman," she said, "are you with us?" Perhaps I stammered a little; I was not with them. I said all I could say, "Excuse me. I was thinking." Without sarcasm, *without sarcasm,* she responded, "Please, don't let me interrupt." And something healed under her deft touch.

On another day, in a room with drawn shades, I saw for the first time the halting Edward Curtis footage of the masked Kwakiutl—a dugout canoe driving forward to the pulled cadence of a drum, all oars in time, a great bird standing in it, beating its wings in time, its big head, massive black beak, menacing. But, of course, it's a silent film; that drum was my heart. Something said yes. As if I had walked by a mirror, not knowing, and, glancing up, recognized who that was floating there in a wall of fluid silver.

In the city, I walk by myself often: in every plate glass window, coming toward me or walking alongside, more me. A crowd of images. The I who walks in the city suffers his own image, in reflection, and in the responses of the people he meets. The more image, the more material he feels. Walking in the woods is a very different thing. The I recedes, things get fluid, the lost magic returns. In the city I am oppressed, but I am oppressive, too.

Once, in Manhattan, staggering under the burden, I escaped the streets into the cool, muffled halls of the Museum of Natural History. Wandering, I followed the lead of my shoes, striking out into strange territory. In the Northwest Coast Indian Gallery, I came to an abrupt halt, feeling, among the totem poles of the great hall, that I had stepped among the trunks of a dreaming woods. I looked through the image on the glass of the cases, finding in the transformation masks something of myself almost beat out of me by growing up in America.

Extracurricular

When the call came, from a friend with an apartment overlooking the Park Blocks in Portland, I crossed over the Ross Island Bridge and went to see how it would happen. The mayor was under pressure to do something about the antiwar demonstrators occupying the Park Blocks. It was clear what he intended. I hadn't known the police were so many. In the Park Blocks the demonstrators clumped around a white tent. They seemed to believe they were immune, that having a permit to be there made a difference, but maybe some of them understood what was coming and just let it come. The police moved in formation, taking up a position along the curb around one long block. They were decisive, in uniform, wearing riot helmets, dangling their white, forty-inch batons. First a few, then all of them, pulled down their shiny visors. Ordered to disperse, the demonstrators locked arms and sat down; that was the formula. On a signal, the police on one end of the rectangle executed a sweep, rushing forward, swinging the big batons at anyone they could reach. They maintained ranks, arriving at the tent all at once. Having arrived, they used their batons, opening foreheads, cracking knees, jabbing straight to the solar plexus. A few students were arrested, but the police weren't there to arrest; they were there to administer a beating.

I cut through the police line and ran to the tent; I had grabbed a broken movie camera from the couch when I left the house, and I meant to use it, to shame the police or frighten them. I pretended the thing worked, zooming close up on masked police doing their job, many of them enjoying it, I imagined. What face did they hide behind the anonymity of their visors? They executed what city hall wanted, and I am afraid what most of the citizens of my hometown wanted. I don't believe my camera did much in the way of calling up a conscience, but it did elicit some attention: I had to dodge away, and I suppose I was lucky not to have been clubbed. I remember seeing a couple of my friends from Reed in the tumult that erupted once the peace was broken—one looking cynical and happy, the other somber; that was Adam.

I went home a few days later. In the old neighborhood they believed what they heard on TV and read in the paper, that the police responded to violence, that what looked like blood was ketchup that the demonstrators had craftily daubed themselves with for the cameras. The mayor lied. For the most part, the local media accepted the lie. In the neighborhood perhaps they had to believe. But on the Park Blocks you couldn't believe, not ever. Before anybody suspected, it was already too late.

Even those of little faith have some faith yet to lose. The real itself, at least the story of the real, begins to erode; and when the stories go, the struggle with what happens begins in earnest. Then odd things happen.

I remember I had taken up meditation, sitting on a pillow in my dorm room all those years ago. One evening my roommate got up, walked down the hall and walked back. I heard him. But he was gone forty minutes, what for me was no time, and I drifted a little farther from the agreed on world. Another night a strange thing happened. I was sitting in a darkened room, thoughtless, afloat on my pillow, and then I was a bird, head turned, looking over a beating wing down on the ocean. To my surprise I spoke, a hoarse croaking, "I'm a bird." Out of the dark I heard the voice of my friend, from where he sat on his cushion, "I see you." Then the door burst open and light flooded the room; a kid I didn't know rushed in, breathless, demanding to know what was going on. He had been in the next room, heard a kind of a song, and without thinking had run to it. I was frightened, that the sirens should sing in my own room!

Under the Holly Tree

When Adam looked me up, my wife and I were living in a basement in Seattle that had last been occupied by a German shepherd. Sometime before that, the walls had been painted with demonic graffiti. We painted them white again and again, but the writhing figures seeped through every coat. We were broke. Work was hard to find, and I was not good at finding it. I didn't know how to want what I was supposed to want.

One day Adam just turned up. I hadn't seen him for two

years. His sudden appearance surprised me; his appearance surprised me. He wore rags. He had stitched together whatever came to hand, adding at the sleeves and cuffs, for he was very tall. I can still see the sandals made of old tires bound up with colored yarns. Yet, standing at the door, there was nothing clownish about Adam. There was a dignity in his carriage; he wasn't proud of his clothes; he didn't notice them. The bike he had dropped in the yard had been patched together from several bikes, the frame soldered and the handles for the brakes fashioned from wood. Yet it was this bike that he had ridden back and forth across the Cascades, crisscrossing the mountains, from northern California to Seattle. It was summer and hot; we sat on a bench under the holly tree in back of the house. There was a garden there, but the sun had turned the clays of that soil hard as pottery.

I can remember only a little of what we said that day. What remains is Adam's unforced earnestness and a sense of sweetness. There was only one Adam. The abyss that yawns for most of us, between who we are and what we do, seemed in him never to have opened. He spoke slowly and without gestures, his eyes turned now to me, now across the parched garden. We talked for hours. I told him I had decided to return to school, that I wanted to teach literature. I remember his face turned slowly toward me, as if swinging on a wide axis, and he asked me if I thought it could be done, to teach and keep my integrity?

It got dark. We tossed his bike in the back of our battered station wagon and drove him home to Shilshoe Bay. The peeling sailboat he lived in was moored among yachts; its cabin was hardly big enough for him to sit, much less stand. All that was in it was a row of books, a lantern, a few blankets. I imagine, for all his gentleness, they—his draft board, the world—found him stubborn, uncompromising. He was uncompromised. People who met him remembered their losses, what they had to give up to be adult. For those who wanted to remember, knowing him was a glorious thing. Some people want to forget.

* * *

After that, we wrote back and forth, letters struggling to address the how of living. I trusted him to call me down from the airy heights, to see how an idea looked muddy. In the end, he was living in a converted turkey-egg incubating hut, finding, I imagine, the accommodations good enough. I wrote again. That letter was answered by his mother. It said, "Our beautiful Adam died this year, worn out from fighting the world." It's the kind of thing we're told happens. But maybe it is done.

Dead Totems

And peacocks in Koré's house,
or there may have been.

—E. P.

Before

Her appearance on the road seems premonitory now. Then, it just seemed incongruous. We were a lot of miles from anywhere, in deep forest, in the coast range of Oregon. It was beginning to get dark. She was standing in the middle of the one lane of blacktop—a peahen, not looking as out of place as she was but definitely one lost bird. We pulled to a stop, having a look. Nothing so beautiful as the unexpected: her neck iridescent as a rainbow, as the iris of a shining eye, her tail flashing green and gold and trailing behind her. After a while, we eased our dark car forward; she began to walk down the road in front of us, leading us down, but not getting off the blacktop. When we sped up, she sped up. She plain refused to take to the woods. I stepped out of the car to shoo. She let me get close. I even considered taking her in my arms—but then what? She was not *for* catching. Anyway, she loped away, her head bobbing at the end of that beautiful, undulating neck. Somehow camel-like in its moving, that neck, I thought insanely, starting to run. Soon I was flapping my arms and squawking, and only then did I manage to chase her over the road edge into the darkness of the woods. Looking after her, suddenly I felt a little shamefaced, forlorn; but when the dark car drifted up beside me, I got in.

Thessaloniki

Six months later I was in Greece.

I found, walking the streets between my bus stop and the university where I was teaching American poetry, between the old
market and my bus stop, between lunch and dinner, that I was
walking more than I wanted to on Egnatia. Even trying to avoid
it, I came back to it—the city courses down it, has done so for
over two thousand years. The traffic is heavy day and night, a
rush of cars, buses, and loud motorcycles, all that noise echoing
against the buildings that line it. Here, the depth of the human
occupation is everywhere apparent—a little chapel that used to
stand flush with the road is now half lost in a hole—there are
whole eras in the basements of these buildings.

Near that sunken (and tilting) chapel, where the whine of the
city is as loud as it gets, I met her again: the unexpected peahen.
She was standing in an alley; back behind there was an open
courtyard and another church. She was pecking around, on the
loose, just a few feet from the rushing traffic on Egnatia. I
stopped dead, watching her; my fellow pedestrians pushed on
by, eyes only for what was up ahead. Having seen her once, I
looked into that alley every time I passed, and as often as not she
was there, looking intent, aloof, and ominous.

I asked my colleagues in the English department if they had
seen the peahen on Egnatia. They hadn't. I asked my friends; I
asked my students. For all my asking, I never found anybody
who had seen that bird, although all of them—some of them
every day—walked up and down Egnatia. That peahen looked
as obvious as can be, but maybe not. Everything is obvious once
you see it. At the time, I didn't connect her with the bird that I
had seen out in Oregon a few months earlier.

One day when she wasn't there I poked around in the alley for
quite a while, finding, at last, a small, iridescent feather. It was a
welcome token; I had begun to doubt. In my palm it shone, radiating out from its dark heart, to green, into blue, into blue-violet

at the farthest extremity. It felt like almost nothing, a point with a halo or the brush of eyelashes. And yet it looked like touch, how the hand feels empty, a cool glow.

I like to touch. We handle things; we handle each other. In doing so, we know something. It's hard to say what—it's very hard to say what. Words won't stick to what is palpably there. As long as we live in our touch, we are ecstatic, out of our minds. We reach out, and our hands are lost in an unseen world.

We like to imagine that this is how animals live all the time. In Greece, I was in a world of sirens and centaurs, of Pan and satyrs, witnesses that in how we feel the animals come close, can merge with us, that beyond the neatness of our thinking there are forces to be reckoned with. We sense it, sometimes, how a foot shades into hoof, an arm into a wing.

Ephesus

At the far side of the archaeological site there is a back door, and like the gate where I had entered there was a little carnival of selling going on there. I was thirsty and looking for something to drink before I turned back into the white streets of the ruined city. A young man at a counter selling Cokes whispered, as he counted out change, "I have a friend working on the dig at Ephesus; silver, he found silver. I show you."

"Sounds like trouble to me," I muttered, turning away, but over my shoulder I heard his whisper loud almost as a shout, "Mister, I have a marble hand . . ."

I walked back into the ruins, unsettled a little by that desperate whisper, walking at random. At the end of the long alley to the sea, or where the sea had been before the port silted in, a boy glided to my side, hoping to sell me some coins, some old coins his mother had dug up in the garden. I sat down beside him on a marble slab, as he was a beautiful boy—dark, a small scar between his eyes, a light neckerchief tied around his throat.

Over his sorry shirt and trousers he wore a not-too-dirty linen sport coat. He coaxed, putting in my hand, one after another, Greek coins, some silver. These he bounced on the marble so I could hear them ring. He fished more coins out of his pockets, tied in small parcels with strips of cloth or wrapped in crinkled foil. I tried to explain the Antiquities Act to him but he wasn't having it. He understood the economy of the situation, seen from his side. His father, he explained, worked on the digs for twenty thousand Turkish lira. "That is nothing," he said. "Every day things cost more, six thousand one day, eight thousand the next." The coin in my hand was beautiful, a little nymph or a goddess, a grace in the palm of my hand. I was tempted.

I told the boy, Ali, that if he would show me the old port I'd give him two dollars. Off we went into tall brush, old columns scattered about everywhere, toward the sea. Fifty or maybe a hundred yards later he pointed to what was left to look at and said, "Here." Great marbles with bulls in low relief. "Here," he said again, stomping the ground, "feel the water"; and I could—the ground responded like flesh. "Water, maybe one meter down." On the walk back, Ali insisted on showing me more coins, stopping here and there to bounce a silver coin on a rock. Who knows, I thought, they might be real. I told Ali I liked his coins, but that I didn't think I should buy one.

"Should?" he asked. "What is should?" I began to explain but it made me feel old and I gave it up. I handed over the two dollars, and his eyes darkened. "My uncle," he complained, pointing to a scowling presence on a rock, "will say I am a bad boy."

After hours amid the white remains of Ephesus, the marble statuary in the museum at Selçuk got boring quick. I retreated into an empty courtyard, hoping to shake the leadenness from my head. But it wasn't empty; there was a peacock out there. When I sat on a low wall, he opened his fan, six feet of blue and green and gold radiance. He came close, his face within inches of mine, and I thought I could see myself in the reflection of his eye (the Koré). He began to scratch his feet on the flagstones in an ecstatic dance. A tremor ran through his whole body as he shook out his tail feathers, a rustling fan. It was so thin it blew over me like a wave in the light breeze—lovely blues of the neck and legs—Mediterranean blues. Then I recognized the dusky orange feather stuck in with the pens on my desk at home, which had been there for years and which I had taken for a dyed turkey feather, as from the wing of a peacock, and he closed his fan.

There was no one else in the garden, a moment out of the crush, the murmur of voices from the museum like soft waves breaking on a distant beach.

The Holy Mountain

We were making a slow exit from Simonos Petras, a monastery on Mount Athos. I had taken shelter from the cold wind behind a stone wall, huddled up in the sun. I was only half listening to the monk, Theophanou, answering questions. I was sunk in the sun, in a kind of stupor, remembering how the day had begun. Sometime in the night, night was over. Somewhere in the darkness a monk had ranged through the monastery carrying an oak board over his shoulder, the *semantron*, which he had beaten rhythmically, and the bells had pealed. The door had opened, and an old monk in the habit of a crow had stuck his beard in at the door, surveying the startled pilgrims severely in the sudden light. Nothing had been said, the door had been pulled shut, and day had begun.

In the predawn gloom the ceremonies had seemed unending. The dark frescoed walls had brightened a little as candles passed, and monks had shuffled in and out, taking shape and losing it as they had come now into illumination, now gone out of it.

In the murky light the gold auras of the saints had shone, the dark features of their faces suffused in gloom. The martyrs suf-

fer still. It did not seem good to me that on Athos spirit is win-
nowed from the soil of the flesh, that the martyrs are saints, the
saints martyrs. Hard for man to join again what God has put
asunder.

I mused on, thinking again how odd it was to have come all
this way to find that Theophanou had attended the same college
in Oregon that I had, and now this is it for him. My companions
were pressing him on the subject of relics, and he was uncom-
fortable, but he noted, with circumspection, that at Simonos Petras they had the left hand of Mary Magdalene and the left hand
of John the Baptist. Later, at Dionysiou, the guestmaster would
recite the relic list with considerably more fervor; there they had
the right hand of John the Baptist "and many other right hands."
He explained that some, miraculously enough, still have the skin
attached. He insisted that something of the sanctity of the saints
inheres in this skin, and that such hands are especially potent. I
looked away, across the terraced gardens to the sea. Two gulls
were trailing over the wake of an orange caïque, a black-robed
monk at the tiller.

Agios Germanos

Hurt Hawks
—R. J.

It seemed a moment of unpleasantness only in a luminous day—
the pelicans on the Prespa Lakes, the Jolly Girl serving us trout
in a lakeside taverna, the radiant heat from the stove, the yellow
light finding and loving the oil on the plate of red peppers.

We had taken a turn, on whim, up a dirt road to Agios Germanos. Everywhere cut bamboo or something like it had been
piled in rough stacks. Jim drove slowly in the narrow lanes. It
was the kind of place tourists travel for, totally "unspoiled." It
was hard to remember what century we were living in; it could

have been anytime but our time. Still, the place was forbidding, seemed only half-inhabited, a Brueghel painting without many people in it. Finally, turning right down an alley lined with stone walls, we came upon the workers; in their hands, hooked knives flashed, and the cane was rendered into stakes. They had a chapped look, wind-reddened, and they looked unfriendly. For the first time in Greece, I felt distinctly unwelcome. It was oppressive: faces so dour they seemed to darken the sky and pull it down.

We drove on, descending. I asked Jim to stop the car on the side of the road, at the edge of town; a hawk had been impaled and made to stand in warning to its kind, its wings pulled out wide and fastened to a cross-stake, sad head hanging over its streaked breast. Crucified out among the chickens. I wanted to have a good look, make my heart accept this, too. All around, the red chickens pecked, taking no notice of me or that hawk.

It seemed only a dark smudge on a bright day. I indulged in a few black speculations on the subject of "manunkind," but that is all. Home through the gloaming—in late dusk by orchards with trees powdered all in blue dust, blue trees ghostly against the dark earth as we swept by.

Thasos

Some walks have a rhythm, a lovely rhythm. The walk up and out of Limenas on Thasos is like that. There is the old agora looking untended, marble in the living green, then the little temple to Dionysus, sunken below the current level of the town. From there, the walk up commences, winding to let you know it's steep. The trail straightens out and runs into a pine grove, between old stone walls, and you're onstage, the stage of a Roman theater. Pines have been allowed to grow among the benches, and there is something inclusive about this, something heartening. On the other side of a gate latched with a twist of wire, the trail turns sharply, up the ridge. The sea is on both sides now—steeply below on the left, through thicket, and over the town on the right, beyond the quiet harbor. It's a soft incline, through the evergreens. There is a little chapel on the left, a single small room with icons and oil lamps burning; then on up, on top now, through the gray ruins of a medieval fortress, where things are kept close cropped by goats. Then it's down and up to the marble foundations of a temple to Athena, wonderful dressed stone. Just beyond that there is a niche cut in the native rock where shepherds worshipped Pan.

A walk like this is a progressive revelation, an uncovering of the heart; I had done it before and was happy to be doing it again. And right there, right in front of Pan's little sanctuary, I walked under the martyred gull. It had been hung from an olive tree with a thin white cord. Its gray wings were drawn up, its white body and head left to hang down. The feet were closed, limp, the yellow beak open wide.

Halicarnassus

By the time we got to Bodrum it was hot—summer had rolled over the landscape. Walking had become a passing from shade to shade. Even the camels on the waterfront, there to remind tourists that they were in Turkey, looked ready to faint. The tomb of Mausolus is just around the harbor, a short walk, but we didn't go. It's the original mausoleum. I ought to have wanted to see it but didn't—enough of the dead. We ate late, at tables hung over the sea. To the east, the lights of the city's big disco shone intermittently, getting ready for the night's show. To the west, the medieval castle of the Knights of Saint John occupied the heights at the jaws of the harbor. A dark woman at the next table, a raven-haired woman, suggested I visit the castle. It was an odd conversation; we sat back to back, and except for an initial and occasional turn to acknowledge that we had bodies, she spoke looking away, just a hushed voice in what had become the night. "Go," she said, "if only to see the peacocks."

We were there the next morning when the gates opened. There was a bin of seed for feeding the birds. I filled my cupped hand with it, with "pulse," as H. D. had taught me to call it. When I held my hand, palm up, out to the strutting bird, he came for it. Inquisitive eyes, eyes everywhere in his fan. When he began to feed, I was surprised at how hard he struck; his head steady, looking, and then the beak flashing into my palm with a percussive shock.

Thessaloniki Again

Just off Egnatia, in a bent alley behind a church and near the university, there is an odd shop I sometimes visited in Thessaloniki. The left wall is all shelves and stacked right to the ceiling with antique kilims from Thrace. The place smells like a goat, and I liked it. When the owner saw me eyeing old votive plaques from churches, in a glass case, he dug out a cigar box full of them for me to rustle through. Some were silver; most were tin, small metal sheets that had been hammered on dies. Every one had for design some part of the body—an eye, an ear, an arm, or a leg. They had been hung from icons by the faithful to signify what needed fixing. I was disturbed by their sad beauty, but a box of them is also macabre, like bodies dismembered. At the very bottom I found a copper hand—the only copper in the box—a right hand, like the one I am writing with, and I bought it, for touch.

Somehow I had been out of touch. From the beginning I had known the dead birds were important to me, that there was something heraldic about them, that they spoke to me of something human and cruel that I must never forget. I had had to look at what had been done, at the open beaks and stiff tongues, eyes gone dull. It was later, when I was talking about the martyred birds *without knowing why*, that it hit me. I say *hit me*, a hard sucker punch, a low blow. The gull and the hawk, they were *my birds*, the private totems of my hidden life, and they had been put to death, and dead, exposed to the elements. Just these two. Of all the birds in Greece it was these two I had stumbled on, martyred.

I was in touch now. I shut up, trying to absorb the blow, trying and failing to get my next breath. I had imagined the dead birds were a reminder of something constant in human nature, about human unkindness, but now they spoke of change, of a change in me. Some things were dead in me, irrevocably past, and suddenly I knew it.

After

I was all the way home before the peacocks made their belated, sweet appearance in my consciousness, before I understood that they had come to replace the hawks and gulls. I had pulled my black car into the driveway, had stopped. Sitting there, I remembered. Often it seems that we live in an economy of losses, that we just go on losing. Yet there is always something more to lose, and I sometimes wonder where that surplus comes from. For a moment I felt it, that the surplus rains on us as gifts. We are always receiving, even as we lose those things that are going from us. Still, I didn't know what to make of peacocks. I was used to my hawks and gulls, dull birds that mean business. Peacocks! Pretty much the showiest birds on the face of the planet. When I got out of the car I was shaking my head. In a gesture pretty histrionic for me, I threw my hands up in mock despair, directly into the sun.

※ ※ ※

At my desk, I read fitfully about my peacocks, hoping to discover what the bird might portend for me. I read how the peacock was Hera's bird and Juno's and how the association with the mother, the goddess, brought the bird into disrepute in Christian times, refashioned it into a bird of ill-omen. I remember the peacocks of my childhood, unhappy birds kept in a run out of sight behind a small house on our street, by a family none of us ever knew. The peacocks were never in view; we surmised them from their terrible, tormented cries. I think about the peacock's slow dancing, as I saw it in Selçuk, from under a wave of shining eyes, that ecstasy. An impulse not to hunt nor to scavenge but to pure display, to unfold what is in one's nature, is nature. I am looking, in all this, for the blessing hand, looking but not finding it.

Perhaps it is there, obvious as anything, hanging in the air above me, but I don't see it. In this I am disabled by the culture I have read my way into, a culture that keeps the animal powers at a distance. Who is there to ask about dead totems, how to bury them, or about how to receive the shimmering peacock? We live in a world where science knows better, where it is only money that changes hands. And yet something persists in darkness and in yearning, where desire hums as an absence. Beyond understanding, I am coming to accept.

In the Attic of Memory

May 1990

It's spring. I've been thinking about traveling, making plans, one imaginary journey after another dreamed over the maps. I have a taste for the dreaming but no faith in the plans. It won't happen as I imagine it. Perhaps it will rain where it was blue sky I looked for, and I will come to know mud or a new smell in the desert. And even then I won't know if it's the smell or the mud that will stay with me, will remain when the story of what happened drops away. The journey isn't over when the bags are unpacked.

I have sat with memory, attentive, not to what I can call up but to what comes uncalled. Such memory is close to dream, sometimes is half made of dream, and, like dream, beneath the notice of the world's business. I do not ask of memory, why this? Why remember the combs heavy with honey in my grandfather's attic, from a time when I was so small I had to crawl to them? I do not ask, what does it mean? I nod, say yes—that is the way to respond to memory, a great solvency, memory again and again.

I have listened to the planners tell of their journeys, their straight narratives, their disagreements about what happened next, as if what happened next was a point of honor. I have wondered at the shape they give memory, or if maybe they hold to the story of their trip to contain, perhaps even to exclude, the way it comes back at them, unprompted, suggestive. I have seen the planners' props, the photographs in albums, chronologically arranged, so they need only turn the page for the next "and then."

This spring I have been remembering summer 1972, traveling in those yellow and white lands that look out on the blue Mediterranean. What is remembered? At Corinth, a rubber sandal, a thong, loosened by the griddle-hot agora, giving way again and again, and me, never able to stop my right foot from following through, stepping down on the burning flagstones. That is memory; it has the real feel. Cooking an omelette on a steep, shingle beach north of Brindisi, the roar of the waves pulling back into the blinding light. The smell of oleanders at Epidaurus. These things come back.

When in Rome (First Night Out)

At midnight we heard a key turn in the dark and sat up. The door swung open, and in the hall light a hand reached in, found the switch, and turned on the overhead. We squinted, dazzled. Loud Italian explanations. There was a woman, standing at our bedside, gesticulating, talking first to us then to the two sleepy men in T-shirts she directed to the cot-sized bed pushed against the wall. Our luggage was removed to the floor, and the bed went up, a cloud floating over us in the big hands of the men. It passed over the horizon at the door. Last Italian explanation. We had planned to stay on but didn't.

Touring in Greece: Tragic Shoulders

The road swung right and then straightened out. There was trouble up ahead. A semi had pulled onto the shoulder, and the driver was running back along the road toward an accident. As we rolled up to it, we could see what it was: there was a horse down. It had been pulling a heavy wagon, out of which a man and a woman were climbing down. She was in tears. Her husband must have beaten the horse, driving it up the steep track to the crossing. The uncoiled whip still trailed from his hand. Hadn't he seen the semi? We couldn't tell, but the horse had been clipped and was down in the gravel, tangled in the traces, spasmodically churning its great legs. The husband cursed the horse—it was Greek but we knew it was cursing. We rolled by, only to meet the running driver, arms pumping, coming down, his face a reflection of the downed horse.

We left our camera under the seat, but memory remembers what it pleases. It's no good to say, "forget it." It's not where the priestess sat poised on her tripod at Delphi that I remember, nor where the birds were read at Dodona, but the face of the truck driver running, the spasms of the horse dying on the road's gravel shoulder.

Mycenaean Moments

We groaned at the sight of the parked tour buses at Mycenae, then struggled up the great ramp to the citadel. The cut-stone walls struck us as the masonry of giants, and for a while we forgot we were not alone. We had come to see the Lion Gate and were for once properly stunned—the elevated weight of the triangle of lions, standing atop a massive stone lintel and gate posts. The whole thing built into the cyclopean fortifications of the citadel, which walled out everything except what we could see through the gate as we approached it—a distant, dome-shaped hill with two triangles of blue sky astride it.

We had stopped, dumbstruck, a moment broken soon enough by the swarms of tourists coming down, one group, then another. We had decided we wanted a picture of the Lion Gate and had begun to wait, hoping for a tourist-free moment. Finally, losing patience, I knelt down close to the ground, making use of the swell in the road between my vantage and the gate to bury the chattering tourists below frame while I took the picture. When this photo was developed, I found I had been only partially successful; there was one head left above ground, as if decapitated, lying on the stone flags of the road.

Inside the Lion Gate, at the grave circle of the Mycenaean rulers, we stood over the honeycombed earth, gazing down. In the morning sun the great shafts shrouded obscure bottoms. If there is a proper gesture for such occasions, we didn't know it but stood mute within the circle of standing sandstone slabs, gazing down, listening to the hum of our blood. Down there Schliemann had lifted gold masks from the skulls of the dead. He had been sure.

The beehive tombs at Mycenae vault high overhead, the walls dressed in stone blocks. Over the door an open triangle echoes the carved stone triangle of lions on the city gate. Looking in, it's a shiny blackness; looking out, all light.

At Mystras

We drove by Sparta and the sparkling Evrotas without a sidelong glance, headed for the Byzantine knob, Mystras, which rose out of the Spartan plain. We had met a friendly Greek soon after we entered the country, told him of our plans, and he had said, "No, no, go see Meteora, go see Mystras." We had never heard of either one, were only vaguely aware that lives had been lived in Greece between classical and modern times. Still, the young Greek's certainty proved stronger than our plans, so we went, all eyes. Mystras seemed deserted the day we were there, but baked to a lovely brown. Small, wonderful churches and monasteries, familiar, nothing like the reaching cathedrals of Europe. And photogenic. But what I remember is how hungry we got, climbing out of the cypresses, up to the fort, clambering all over. I was delighted when we came upon a big fig tree, with ripe fruit visible, high but not too high in its branches. I passed the camera to Ellen and began to climb, happily harvesting the wrinkled fruit as I scrabbled from limb to limb. Just as I finished picking enough for a meal, I heard an angry buzz below. A lively old nun had emerged from the adjacent building and was scolding me, I think, for a thief, and I was. The photogenic building beyond the wall, I could see from my vantage in the tree, was not abandoned, not purely picturesque, but was a living convent. I climbed down awkwardly with one hand full of sticky figs and a load of chagrin. I offered up the figs, looking into her black eyes, at her scowling face. She refused them, turned away, and left me the supplicant.

At Meteora

At the turn off to Meteora, we bought a round watermelon and split it on the spot—lunch, sticky. I remember the steering wheel was tacky under hand as I drove the twists and bends up valley to Meteora. It's a gigantic landscape: towering stone spires, many hooded with monasteries inhabited nearly a thousand years. They are perched precariously, high up, some of them accessible only by rope ladders or foot bridges thrown out over precipice. They were the most beautiful buildings I had seen, built on unassailable sites with what must have been terrific, arduous labor. Of Meteora, I remember most vividly not the monasteries but crawling down the road's gravel shoulder into the brush to get a thistle into the foreground of a photograph. It's a fine photograph, but I remember taking it, not seeing the monastery that was my subject.

Into the Sea

The overnight passage to Crete was rough, waves up and sky threatening. Our tickets were good for the deck only, so we spread our sleeping bags downwind of cover and rolled with the ferry. There was a party somewhere below, but when the Mediterranean began to heave in earnest the celebrants fell silent. Later we heard several choking at the railings, and by dawn we were glad to have slept on deck—the passenger compartments below were awash in vomit. In the morning light we ate plums and a small, heavy loaf of Greek bread and watched Crete rise from the sea. We were led ashore by gulls, the big ferry groaning as it eased into the slip. That evening, settled in a cheap hotel in Iraklion, we began to plan what we would do on Crete. We had bought a guidebook, and reading the bloody history of Crete, I remembered how Nikos Kazantzakis, the patron saint of our travels, had almost been a victim of the island's struggles, how his father had instructed wife and children that if the marauding Turks came to their door, he would kill them first, to deprive the enemy of that pleasure.

The guidebook almost promised we would see no rain in our week's stay, it rained so rarely. But the next instant we heard the distant cannonade of an approaching thunderstorm, which was soon enough upon the city. Together we jumped up—it looked like a good time to visit Kazantzakis's grave. We drove the streets at random, calling to Cretans taking cover, asking them one after another, "Where is the grave of Kazantzakis?" We found the spot but were dismayed to discover that the grave site, which stood atop a bastion of the old Venetian wall, was closed for the night. The stern signs of the dictator, Papadopoulos, bright in the lightning, warned against trespassing. We examined the fence—chain link, about eight feet high. It still seemed like a good time to visit Kazantzakis's grave, so we scaled the fence, jumping down with a whoop, taking the way up to the grave. We located it without difficulty, surprised to find it marked with a cross. We

jaw. A great grief descended on me, and a horror, a grief for all the living, for the whole and the maimed alike. Stumbling, my sense of direction ebbing away, I climbed on, leaving the cobbled road for the hillside itself, climbing up through olives and brush toward the hilltop above. With every step I seemed to lose my way, and when I arrived on top, I was lost and exhausted. I sat in the afternoon sun, listening to the birds and the crickets, to human voices carried on the wind, my mind silent now. I had been delivered, but only delivered from, not to.

I started down into the dusty town. Swallows turned in the blue air, then bats. I found our room without difficulty, mounting the stairs with heavy feet. Inside, my wife still slept. I bent over her clear brow, over the sinuous lines of her face, and grieved, remembering that other, maimed face, and grieved for my own wife in her living.

And Then (*Story Maybe Overcomes Memory*)

The Basilica of Saint Francis sat heavily on its haunches, its stone rising out of the stone cobbles of Assisi. At the door we considered not going in. We were dressed for church visiting. Even in the morning coolness we were beginning to heat up, and that, as much as anything, pulled us across the threshold into the obscurity of the church.

I was not amused to discover a souvenir stand manned by Franciscan brothers in the basilica itself. I tried to imagine what Francis would have said to this and could not. Speechless, I lifted our camera from my wife's arched neck and approached the brother who was offering an American housewife a crucifix. He leaned across his wares, crucifix cupped in one hand, the glittering chain draped across to the other. It was an oily gesture, oozy. I took offense; I took his picture. The monk stood up, eyeing me uneasily; the housewife looked scandalized. I lowered the camera. The monk resumed, again unctuously leaning over

the cradled crucifix. I took his picture again, grinning wildly as
he straightened up, startled; he was beginning to get angry, too.
The woman decided against the purchase and edged away from
the counter. I grinned at the monk, who pretended to ignore
me. One of the faithful, an Italian woman dressed in black,
asked to see an icon. Brother Salesman held it out toward her. I
pressed right up to him, for a close-up, maniacally whispering,
"Good, good." The second customer bolted; I stepped back,
lowered the camera, still grinning. The monk looked by me, sig-
naling to someone behind, and I felt Ellen tug at my sleeve. I
agreed to be led away.

In another room we stood before Giotto's serene painted walls,
so blue, and I cooled down. I thought of Francis preaching to
the birds, not yet betrayed, still fluent in the bird tongue.

Back in the streets of Assisi, I listened to the birds twittering
in the trees, in the dark shade, listened, letting the birds preach
to me. I had no word for them, except inarticulate words of love,
but I had ears for their voices, better voices than I had ever
heard from the rostrum. And I dropped into a dazzling realm
where human voices are not words but calls.

June 1990

I have been excavating in the attic, finding no golden masks but
masks of a sort, our journals from 1972. Reading them, I have
felt as I did as a child, sitting on a box in another attic, reading
my parents' letters from before I was born, barely recognizing
people I thought familiar. We were museum-goers. Our journals
are filled with Goya and El Greco in Spain, *The Burial of the
Count of Orgaz*, in Italy with Michelangelo's *Slaves*, still emerging from the stone, with the emaciated and the half-formed
everywhere, with gargoyles and mermaids, with centaurs and

birdlike sirens. And yet I recall these things now with an act of will. The roadside racks of drying raisins we saw on the drive out are more vivid to me now than the palace at Knossos. The arbor of grapes hanging over our table in a garden restaurant, the half-wild cats begging for scraps, are more vivid than the nearby marble columns at Sounion. Nothing I thought worthy of my journal, nothing, has found a place in living memory. Somehow ashes got into all my plans. Yet I was living, finding what mattered even as I looked away.

Coda

December 1990

We were weary after a day in Canyon de Chelly. We had a room in Chinle at a motel on the edge of town. It was late when I opened the door to look out for the lost hound we'd fed earlier, thinking to give him the last of the bread from the beehive ovens of Acoma. He wasn't there. But there was something there in the dark lot, and I walked barefoot out beyond the car to see what: a little herd of sheep, sleepy-looking but standing bunched up tight. Some were curly horned and, tentatively, butted heads, a quiet clack, and the soft clatter, almost a rustling, of their hooves on the blacktop as a small sheep dog swung around them. He was less than knee high, but he had their attention. He did not bark but silently circled the herd, slowly moving them off, across the parking lot and away. Soon I wasn't sure I could see them; then I was sure I couldn't. But I can still hear their hooves, a soft clatter. Before going back in I broke the bread in bits and threw it out onto the blacktop, for that stray, any stray, or sparrows.

Balkan Walks

I walked. Once, I stopped in front of a window flush with the street. It was night and the house was dark. That starry light shone in the window, and the window itself seemed to swim, fluid, something floating in it slowly downstream. I could almost see myself there, the suggestion of a face like another. "Kevin," I whispered, to remember, then turned away and walked on, down another curving alley, up in old town, with Thessaloniki down below only lights.

Having no destination, I walked without destination and therefore without end.

12 February

Thessaloniki. New to town, I have no place to live. So today I walked. I was called up to the bent streets of the upper city and to a neighborhood called Forty Churches. Thessaloniki is built between the hills and the gulf, so walking at random is comfortable—it didn't seem possible to get so lost that I would never find myself. I walked by day and at night. I want to find a place right there, to float over the city lights but be able to walk to the university to teach when the time comes. But I've been told I'm unlikely to find a furnished flat so close. It's not the convenience, it's the crooked alleys I want, the streets too narrow for two cars to pass, windows on the street and sunken courtyards, private places behind high walls.

I walked slowly on cobbles; an old man crossed the lighted frame of a window wearing an open robe over shorts. He didn't see me passing by. I want to find myself in this world, in neighborhoods that make us meet, face to face, to live.

It was not to be. "My place" was out of town, a long bus ride down the eastern shore of the Thermaic Gulf. In old towns, whatever my desire, I remained outside.

24 February

Kavala. The gate was chained with a padlock. Access denied. I peered through a crack between the door slats of the Imaret, the town's old almshouse, built for three hundred. The place apparently had already fallen from favor when the locals began to call it *Tembel-Haneh* (the Lazy Man's Home). A lazy man myself, I didn't like being locked out and wondered who had let the place fall into such disrepair and if it was laziness or righteousness on the part of the townspeople that let it happen. The shadows were heavy, not much to be seen in there; and I walked on, into the old city where it's clustered around the citadel. A few streets up I looked back. From there the Lazy Man's looked lovely hanging over the town harbor down below, its many gray domes fluid under the gray sky, over the blue sea. The size of the Imaret was not apparent from close in front, where it presents a wall no more imposing than the shops across or on either side of it—and less well kept. The place was never meant to dominate the street, for all its size. It holds no promise but stands like an old memory of a life more at ease.

I hiked on up, turning with the bend of the alleys, to the locked doors of the medieval fort on top. I didn't mind this lock so much; the old town itself was enough, a gift of sudden prospects, echoing walls, buildings turned on the second story to greet the sun. How wrong we went with cities, with square plots and zoning. The defining beauty of these places is in the imaginative response to limiting circumstance, to what was already there, and the supple folk tradition in building that said how. The very pavement—paving stones in one herringbone down the narrow alleys—is beautiful. So much gets lost in trying to be perfect.

What calls out from the houses is not la vita nuova *but another life. The heart is not content to live in just these shoes; it wants to try on another life—there, in summer, in that courtyard behind a green door, under that fig tree, on that rickety bench, sitting in thick fig shade. And many houses call out, and every one says "live here."*

1 March

Melnik. There is less to intrude on the rough stone setting here than perhaps in any settlement I have ever seen. The town seems to be made from the landscape—the roof tiles, from the local clays; the elaborate foundations, from the local stone; unpainted wood only and ironwork left to rust. Melnik speaks the local dialect. Almost every building in the village is whitewashed, only one or two tan ones up above and a single pale blue one in town. Perhaps that one is to call down the sky. The foundations are stone, the courses marked by wood laid in at about thirty-inch intervals, so they look a little striped. Mortar has been pressed between the stones, but still plenty of stone showing. The houses, as in the old town in Thessaloniki and in Kavala, are often asymmetrical but not nearly as crowded (no fortifications to press the city into). The eaves are wood, sometimes a little up-turning or plastered out in graceful, concave curves. Five or six small chimneys float over the tiled roofs, some topped with tiles themselves but many just plastered to a point, with four square holes left in the waist. Almost all the houses are cantilevered out over their tall foundations, dark, untreated wood showing there in an apron around the building proper.

This presents—but quietly, not discordantly—each building to the eye. Even relatively uninteresting buildings proclaim their houseness. The interesting ones are sculptural. The ironwork all through town is outsize: sunbursts around the door pulls, locks too big for the key to ever fit in a pocket. Still a job for a blacksmith here. Corn had been hung to dry, and gourds; there were neat stacks of firewood, stone terracing for garden plots, and vineyards all around—all in accord with the buildings and with the landscape. At the upper end of town the remains of an old church with a small patch of blue fresco in the nave still stands. The blue patch seems somehow to allude to the one blue building down below. I saw no plastic except a little sheeting for makeshift greenhouses, strung over small hoops stuck in the worked earth of the gardens. I saw one bicycle and a few cars, even these painted in earthy colors—nothing discordant. New construction is just like the old, and things falling down are still part of it. Roads peter into goat paths, twisting back and forth up the steep hillsides, every stone solid in place.

Walking outside—never going in, never seeing in a window or a door—perhaps this too gave the place its presence, its wonderful insistence on its solids and objectness. Houses that insist that they are heavy, and things, yet standing. It all seemed timeless but is not; Melnik once was home to twenty thousand, now to about three hundred fifty. There must be rubble everywhere, a substrate beneath the living.

Passing through stills time, stills change.

8 March

Skopelos town is a traditional harbor town, laid out in a maze of narrow streets, some with overhanging balconies, some with steps, some with enclosed walkways arching across from side to side. The roads are inlaid with stones set in cement, with painted borders—the bounding line of public space. I spent hours walking up and around what was really a very compact town. While the layout of the streets was the most mazy I have seen, the buildings themselves were relatively rectilinear, perhaps a little less interesting than those in Kavala. If the streets kept me turned around, the island kids ran with abandon to their destinations, up and around but not away.

I walked a loop around the harbor, crossing the radial streets one at a time. Passing one, I turned when I heard the sound of tramping and wailing cover my footsteps: in the notch between buildings I watched the quick leading the dead down, the casket small enough to be a child's, swinging aloft, a little boat buoyed on the river of the living, flowing down toward the harbor.

All changelessness a dream.

❋ ❋ ❋

Makrinitsa. At the upper end of a switchback road, high up, the town was thronged with Greek tourists, but I made it, walking in past stalled cars under snowy skies. It clings to the hillside, constructed from native slates, rough slate roofs, slate squares and courtyards, slate paths and roads. The slates are mostly green, but some are brown, some gray. The entire town is built of slate and stucco. Here, as at Skopelos, I hiked in the cold, up to churches, down to guesthouses, all around the main square with its big old plane trees. Up and down are decisive here, only the square and one long street run much on the level. And as in the old town on Skopelos, the small terraces and kitchen gardens, the open spaces, though intimate, do a great deal to open things up, to include, finally, the sky.

White pelicans cruised the Prespa Lakes. The stony village of Psarades fronts Big Prespa where it looks into Albania. The water was limpid, a line of fishing boats pulled up on the beach. The town is all stone under tile roofs, buildings not even plastered. Stones for building are everywhere, almost covering the ground or half covering the ground. The next house is there for the building. Some of the places have fallen into rubble, some are well kept, all are beautiful; they seem assembled on the spot from what came to hand, and no doubt they were. The town runs in a strip along the beach; the hills rise up above, stony and beautiful too.

Cows kept wandering right through town, untended, on the streets and in the alleys: something wonderful in the pace of their appearance and disappearance, something like clouds streaming through mountain passes or drifting over lakes.

❉ ❉ ❉

Buildings built from their surroundings, out of the native stuff, have an entirely different kind of authority from that of buildings assembled just anywhere. They seem more animated, as if the living idea that put them up and keeps them standing is more visible in the material, because the material loses itself in the surroundings. Nothing distracts the eye, the heart, from what a house is. I think of the sad suburbs in Portland where I grew up and despair.

It's an irresistible metaphor, what we see in a house that animates its surroundings, with its form, its beauty—something about how a life takes shape, or should.

The best beauty is earthly.

6 April

Walking again the old town in Thessaloniki. It rises above the downtown, a haven over too much concrete housing. The old town is varied, with many things in ruins or near to ruins but also many new places, some in the vernacular style but some not; the old town seems to welcome them all, to include them. It accommodates many neighborhoods, some upscale and kept by the urban young, some housing older, more traditional Greeks, and some veering close to shantytown. Taking a path, away from the noisier streets, I walked up a seam of poor houses, half wonderful, half stricken, where human artifice, the ability to make something out of whatever turns up has sometimes triumphed. There I stepped forward to find myself standing, on a sharp hillside, half in a little manger, where an old white horse, almost filling it, placidly ate from a can hammered to the wall.

✿ ✿ ✿

Some new houses have been constructed right in the ruins of old buildings. I saw one built into a declivity, with one of its walls abutted by the ruins of a medieval wall, the new house curling within the remains of the old—this place in the new style, white with verandas and covered porches, bright varnished wood all about for trim. Another small place has been built entirely within the remains of an old foundation, on a hillside overlooking all Thessaloniki down below, big ships plying the Thermaic Gulf.

The Byzantine city wall looms at the crest of the hill and the castle: great crenelations, ragged teeth, and old arches for passage. A round tower above the city walls, an echo of the White Tower on the waterfront, here floats into stars.

Walking these streets, I fell into a brown study, wondering forever at the color of the walls, one after another—the primrose and the neon blue, the ocher and the umber, white chipped away to reveal old green and that green to reveal a faded pink. Some walls have kept their color where they were shaded in summer, so that summer shade is now remembered in an intensity of color, a flagrant yellow.

I imagined for a long time that Greeks possessed a native gift for color, that only a gift could make such colors sleep peacefully on adjacent walls. But when I looked closely, put my nose to it, I came to understand that some of the colors were not at all attractive. What made them feel right, imperative to the place, were the houses themselves. The gift was not for color but to have such houses to paint.

15 April

Kavala again. I resolved to hike to the castro a second time, to see if the gates might be unlocked this time, but didn't. I

stopped climbing when I noticed that the Imaret had an open
door, which turned out to be the entry to a restaurant of the
same name, built into the decay of the old seminary (not origi-
nally an almshouse at all as it turns out: the Lazy Man was a
scholar!). I loved this restaurant, down in a sunken garden, all
surrounded by pillared porticoes, opening into rooms, and ruins. That the Lazy Man had proven commercial amused me a
bit. This use of ruins, just cleaned up a little, reminded me of the
houses built within ancient foundations in the old town in Thessaloniki. The place has been whitewashed as it opens on the
restaurant, with some mustard walls and trim, but the old rooms
have not been restored—peeling plaster and layer on layer of
paint, blue-domed ceilings a dark sky within. The little walled
garden, sunken in the center of the old complex, is coming back
now, the old trees and vines newly tended, fresh grass planted,
and a few new small trees.

*Another life, taking shape within the slough of the past, its cast.
We not only make ourselves from, we are made from it.* Agere et
pati, *as I learned it in school, to act and to suffer. I sat in the
Imaret drinking my coffee* metrio, *as sweet as I could stand it,
bittersweet.*

To tell no lies is to acknowledge the ragged edges, the rim of decay.

31 May

When the precincts at Dodona closed and I was shut from the
oracle, I moved on to modern Dodoni for a Coke. While I was
drinking it, in the hush of late afternoon, the proprietor told me
that no one wanted to live in the village across the way, also
called Dodoni, because it was too hot. Looking across I could

see that it was laid out on a grid—no trees, no charm, built all at once, the work of bulldozers.

I traveled on, far up into the amazing rocky Zagoria, spaghetti roads to Megalo and to Mikro Papingo—mountain villages, one aesthetic, all stone. In Mikro many of the footpaths are covered by grape arbors now in leaf. Hiking, village to village, is popular here, and it is obvious why! I feel it in my feet: the desire to walk.

The mischief is in wanting it all new.

12 June

Soon I'll be leaving Thessaloniki for good. I walk the upper city a few last times, with affection, as if with love at my side; and the hard lines of my conceptions swim in beauty, a wet brush swept across a watercolor sketch of these places. A home built right into the old city wall, the facade of the house flush with the wall—green shutters. An abandoned lot behind an iron gate and a stairway running up to the threshold of a building no longer there. The click of footsteps in the still air.

15 June

Rhodes. I took a long, leftward-turning walk through the moat around the walled city. Hot sun radiated down the crusader's canyon. Serious fortifications, the teeth of the crenelations cut into the shape of a capital *M*, niches for crossbows everywhere. I can't imagine how foot soldiers must have felt getting the order to charge the walls—their mortality upon them, I guess. The stones are a honey-colored brown and look almost new, but bellicose, only encouraging for those who live within.

The old town inside is touristed on the few main streets, but away from there the alleys turn to accommodate the shape of the walls and the lots: centuries of acquisitions and dispositions—some straight, some not. The land is relatively flat, so the curves don't seem to derive from geometry but from history. Any frustration of the planned, the plotted, is an opportunity for beauty. Here things have taken the shape of living through time.

Many of the doors and windows appear within a blazon of color, the wall itself left in stone or in one or more previous paint jobs. Some walls have been freshly plastered and painted; the doors typically pull up tight behind a curved stone arch. Most have a wreath of dried flowers hung over the door for luck. It's all very private; there are not many courtyards to peer into here. I followed blue and pink walls down one alley, then a tight turn and ocher and tan, then a left and more ocher; there one building extends half its width over the alleyway. Why do I love this? Most of the alleys are made of small beach stones polished to a sheen by the foot traffic.

Whenever the earth itself is moved, a sweet geometry is lost. What's built responds too much to what's in the mind, not enough to what is given in the place. What I fall for is not statement but response, answers to the promise of place.

16 June

Lindos. The town is set in a saddle between the hills of Rhodes and the acropolis where it towers over the sea. Looking down on it, I see that most of the roofs are flat and finished in earth-colored clays—tan, gray, dun, green, or red—with a raised, whitewashed border around the edge. A few have pitched tile roofs. All look totally clean, wind-scrubbed, except for the occasional rooftop restaurant set out in tables.

All the walls of Lindos are whitewashed except for the very

four sketches of houses, every one with neoclassical detail, triangular facades. My heart swam. I seemed to know, if only for a moment, what it would be like to grow up with certainties, to know without thinking what a house should be and how to live.

Hunting on Human Ground

1. For the Birds

It is still raining. Just upstream a family of four kingfishers is perched on a snag over the river, the Frying Pan. I stop casting, letting my fly go with the current: the kingfishers. The young ones are getting fed. They are noisy at table, chittering, but these are formal birds, a lot of bowing going on. Head and tail go down together, then up together. Big-headed birds, all that beak. One by one they fly, resume fishing. I raise my rod tip and flip my line upstream, over the water; I am fishing too.

There are a few green drakes emerging out of the rain-pocked river, but the trout are down, and my attention shifts; now it's the kingfishers, now my line uncoiling in the air over the water, now the red cliffs. Sun's out and the water clear, as if the rain was all illusion or filtered through the red basalt. In a ripply run I catch a good fish, a rainbow, darkly speckled and heavily rouged on the sides. When I put him back he holds still in my hands, gills pumping, his presence as mysterious as a god to me, that other. He edges out of my palms, head into the current; I see him rejoin his shadow near the bottom; then he is gone.

Walking back to the car, I meet a little bird on the roadside.

He's squinting, spun down, I think, by the turbulence of a passing car. I kneel down next to him, offer my hand, and without hesitation he walks up into it; it's three or four steps. He sits, and I carry him down the road cut, away from traffic. When I put my hand down, he walks off, looking unruffled, his pale olive breast rising and falling, just visibly, with each breath.

Back on the water in the evening, caddis flies are returning to the river to lay their eggs, fluttering, mothlike, dapping on the river in the failing light. I am fishing to rising trout, my elk hair caddis also fluttering down here and there. I notice, when my concentration breaks, that when I am really fishing, I am most a heron. My feet get lost under the surface glitter. I remember stalking close to a great blue heron years ago, on Lake Cachuma, over the hill from Santa Barbara, moving half-steps when it looked away, until, at ten feet or so he turned his knifey beak on me, and I saw how thin he looked to a fish, nothing like the menace of his profile when the menace was real.

I stalk now too, bent forward a little at the waist, all eyes and the long arm of my fly rod twitching overhead. The fly goes where I want; the trout are willing.

The day has gone. The bounding light has gone out. I am all hunter now. Wading over river stones by feel, still casting. There are no distinctions; I stroke the air, the river, my fly line snaking out and back. At the end of day, at the end of the line, the Goddard caddis that is fishing finds a last trout.

25 July, Roaring Fork

When an afternoon shower sweeps the river in Woody Creek Canyon, I stop fishing, finding a rock to my liking, under a big

blue spruce, to rest on. I ache; hours of wading in the heavy water of the Fork, over the round and slick stones, is enough for
me. I set about constructing a new leader, tying on a big hair-
wing drake when I'm done. The trout have been on the drakes
all afternoon, very willing. It's been fast fishing: short drifts,
definite takes, wild fighting in white water. I've caught some I
thought I wouldn't, some I despaired of. Things conspire, sometimes, in my favor.

When the rain stops, the swallows return to the river, green-
backed and white-bellied, like the trout feeding on the emerging drakes. Andy wades back in cross river, then Ellen. She
works out a little line, then casts, her line straightening out over
the river before falling onto a promising current tongue. I go on
watching for a long while, then wade across the river to talk, to
hear their stories.

2. Utah Road Sign: "Eagles on the Highway"

28 July, Sego

They seem to be gods, or shamans, painted in pigments the
color of dried blood. They loom on the cliffs at Sego. They have
been here a long time. They were looking down on the Frémont
Indians when they pecked their glyphs on the same cliffs, maybe
a thousand years ago; on the Utes when they painted the live
rock in the nineteenth century; and on the Anglos, who came after. Barrier Canyon figures like these are old, but present, too.
Most of the archaic forms here are limbless, floating torsos,
faces featureless but for the circles that are eyes. Their heads are
hieratic, adorned with horns or feathers. A thin figure is flanked
by two standing snakes, one at each shoulder, as if imparting secrets or getting wisdom.

On another clean stone face, a bison-headed pictograph
seems to twist its neck in horror. I can't know the original occa-

sion for that look, but there are occasions enough. Today, in the dust of the arroyo not five feet away, I find a deer leg, gnawed off at the knee. Recently, very recently, this hoof tracked the wash, these hills. Now it is detached. I don't want to be.

It's clear, at Sego, that in the end, at whatever speed, the human print is going. An old bridge has washed out in the canyon, the pictographs and petroglyphs are giving way to weather, bullets, and graffiti; and the green signature, "Sip and Glenna Farley, 10-11-14," although it looks fresh as yesterday, is going too. It's curious, that on the blank pages, where no Barrier Canyon artist, Frémont or Ute, has written, there is no graffiti either. It's as if our fathers and our mothers required a spur, felt the need to assert their culture only in the face of other cultures, and, sadly, all they had to assert were their names, identity at the minims.

I ponder the rows of human figures, with arms held up or joined as if in invocation, and think again of the loneliness of a name: Sip Farley. But if many of the glyphs, as some suggest, are clan signs, perhaps the impulse behind them is not so different, is also a naming. And I see where the Frémont have chipped their figures over more archaic ones and where the Utes have painted theirs over Frémont. I want to see them as all alike, for all of us to join arms, but I can't; my eyes are all for the Barrier Canyon and Frémont work.

Kingbirds are working the air overhead as I examine the small Frémont glyphs, somehow both static and lively, with their trapezoidal torsos, wide shoulders tapering down not to feet but to a pin or a pivot. These figures wear complicated necklaces and earrings; their "bucket" heads are elaborately adorned. They stand forth, dominion from the rock.

Near Moab

(Same day)

At sunset we watch rock climbers scale cliffs over the Colorado near Moab, cliffs bearing the Frémont signature everywhere.

The climbers are calling back and forth about the difficulty of the ascent. A small bat flits in the gloom—now grappling on the cliff face, now casting off to hunt—for mosquitoes, we realize all at once.

The brown Colorado—how hard it is for me to say yes to it, having grown up with clear water, loving clarity, realizing late the need to love mud.

29 July, Canyonlands

In over thirty miles of dirt into the trailhead at Barrier Canyon (aka Horseshoe), we see no one, but there's a ranger's truck at road's end. The trail down is over slick rock, the live stone of the canyon, marked only by occasional cairns or small rocks set in rows. We reach the canyon floor, a level wash, just as what turns out to be three rangers are readying to climb out. They tease Ellen and me about being here today—it's 110 in the shade— and seem to doubt we'll make the six miles in and out.

Walking in the wash is harder than I imagined, much of it gives way at a footfall, and that's tiring. And although we are drinking often, we are always thirsty. But I don't doubt we'll make it. We walk, listening to Raven talking in the canyon.

The figures at the High Gallery, like the Barrier Canyon pictographs at Sego, are a rusty, blood red. One is a winged human, shaman, or god, wings out. Is it the bird in the human, the human in the bird, or the bird and the human in the god, that here finds expression? It does not fly but walks or dances, a little awkwardly, like Raven on the ground. Across the canyon, on a second panel, there is an upright snake, talking, or perhaps a snake with a bird's head, but certainly talking.

❀ ❀ ❀

The pictographs at the Alcove, though large, are dwarfed by the stone amphitheater in which they appear, a great mouth opened in the wall of the canyon. We sit inside, cool in the shade that must have been constant from the time of the painters to our time: millennia. The figures run in a band, and here there is little graffiti, though Bub Vance, in 1904, and Sadie Vance, in 1928, wanted us to know they were here. We rest, looking out at the cottonwoods, pulled down onto their sides by flash floods but still growing. Walking upwash, I saw cottonwood leaves turned a green metal and brittle, dried mud broken into tiles. I drink— water tastes good in dry places—and pass the jug. Ellen drinks too, her face drawn in need and pleasure.

Behind the rubble in the Alcove stands a three-foot horned man. He's lively and clownish, a little snicker among the other overwhelmingly forbidding Barrier Canyon figures. He is the trickster on my shoulder, ready to laugh at things going well, at things going badly.

The hike up to the Great Gallery, as the rangers had it, is "to heck and gone." The sun ripples in the wash, molten; Raven croaks in the heat waves. Consciousness itself runs. When I cough, it rolls back in staccato echoes. On a sandy patch I find a dead mouse, his small fingers curled into his palms. I do not think he wanted this.

The Great Gallery is painted on a shady wall. Sitting under cottonwoods, under specters, I am stunned that anything painted could assert itself against the sheer presence of this stone canyon, against heat and thirst; I shake my head; these figures do. Any thought that the fixed presence of the watching figures, of the one called the Holy Ghost, is a deficiency of technique rather than intent is dispelled by a nearby hunting scene. Here, two men with spears and a dog hunt a dozen desert rams.

The hunters, fully articulated, a little elongated, show their spears in a dance of attention while the dog drives the rams to them. I know that dance. I find it when I fish with my fly rod, attending, and hiking these arroyos, watched over, like the hunters on the wall, by still and ghostly presences.

30 July, Capital Reef

At Fruita we walk the paths by the orchards where the Frémont Indians chipped their glyphs over the river. It's called the Frémont River now, after the explorer John C. Frémont; and the culture that wrote on these walls is called the Frémont, after the river. Whatever they called themselves is long lost.

An irrigation channel cut from the river runs along the base of the canyon wall and on into the settlers' orchards. Such channels might have watered the corn and squash of the Frémont, too, but now the channel serves as a barrier, to keep tourists from defacing the petroglyphs. I dip my foot in it, cold; I call it good, real wealth in the desert.

There is a bear pecked in a wall at Fruita. It is the only Frémont bear I have seen, though prints of the bear clan appear often. I am deeply impressed by this figure, its simple angular beauty, and struck by the similarity, perhaps even identity, of its lines and the lines of the bear figures carved by Eskimo in the far north.

On the way back to the car I see a doe walking in the orchards, the garden, and I remember Lorine Niedecker on Wintergreen Ridge—Lorine remembering too:

> Every creature
> better alive
> than dead,
> men and moose
> and pine trees

And I embrace this, kiss it, yet I know I am a hunter and forget it at my peril.

3. Poor Fishing

31 July, Dutch John

The man behind the counter looks glum when I ask how the Green is fishing. If anything, keepers of fly shops tend to lie on the happy side, so I prepare for poor fishing.

The trout in the Green are large and visible as we hike down off the bluff below Little Hole in the late afternoon. I like to fish on top; in fact, I fish dry flies pretty much all the time. Watching—sometimes watching for—a fly on a moving river is mind stilling; and in the silence of that attention the fisher emerges, heron-headed, a little splay-footed, gawky.

The wind picks up, and the light begins to go. I am fishing the water, the edges of current tongues, behind rocks. There are no takers until it's almost too dark to see; when the big trout strikes, I hear as much as see him slash at my Madame X no more than a foot from shore. He fights well, takes me down two riffles before I net him in slack water. Heavy-bodied, broad across the back, he wears the war paint of a cutthroat. He pulses in my hands and is gone, back out into the glassy currents of the Green. Hiking the mile and a half back to Little Hole in the dark, I am lulled, almost to dreaming, by the glowing dry grass, like a lunar fog, that sweeps around the few junipers on the bluff top. So little of fishing is fishing.

1 August

The next afternoon we head up the Green from Little Hole in the carnival atmosphere that commonly prevails on this stretch of the river. Rafts of girls sweep by, singing, "Row, row, row your boat, gently down the stream, merrily, merrily, merrily, merrily, life is but a dream." I reflect again on what an odd little round this is for children to sing, all about the floating world, maya, and remember my own enthusiasm for it when I was in grade school. But now I'm planning to fish: hoppers or cicadas against the bank to holding trout, trout that are real enough for me.

I hunch down on a rock not five yards below a large brown—I can see his gill covers open and shut, the occasional beat of his fins as he holds his position on the bottom. Ellen observes that it doesn't look promising: he's not feeding. Still, with a slight twitch of my rod I send my hopper into the water about a foot in front of him and six inches off to his right; it lands with a light plop. No response. I try again, this time a little to the left of him. As the current brings it even with his left eye, I give it a little action, to simulate a struggle, and he turns and takes. I strike, and the fight is on; he runs deep, twisting, coppery in the green current, then jumps once. Soon he's thrashing on the surface, and I slip my net under him. It's an old male, with a hooked snout. When I put him back, he swims slowly for the middle of the river.

It's a good start to a slow day. Hiking upstream, beyond the pocket water to the larger holes, I see that the trout have begun to midge; I'm ill-equipped for that kind of fishing, so I call it a day, enjoying the hike back along the big river in the dry canyon.

2 August

I have heard a rumor that fishing is better down at Brown's Park on the Green, with hoppers and beetles, cicadas and attractors—the kind of fishing I've come for. So we set out on the long road from Dutch John.

Where the highway passes into Wyoming, Ellen and I get out with a napkin map to hunt for a petroglyph panel I've got wind of. Over a ridge and down along its desert-varnished face. After half a mile, we're thinking we turned the wrong way but are happy to have discovered the cowboy inscription "FreD Large" and a fanciful picture: a horseshoe laid on its side with a horse's head emerging from between its legs. Ellen finds the petroglyphs on the way back to the car, and I find a little mouse, hardly bigger than my ring, which I press into the sand next to him for a photograph.

At Brown's Park the river is muddy. I drive by a fishing camp, rod tubes shining where they lean against a tree, the one fisherman staring disconsolately at the river. He doesn't look around as I turn in a U and head back toward Little Hole.

The fish are down, and I wait on a high rock where yesterday we had seen the midging trout, prepared this time, thinking it will happen again. In the run below me, I watch twelve or fifteen trout feeding, occasionally, on nymphs. The longer I watch, the more individual they become, not only in appearance but in their habits. The large red rainbow just below me chases off any trout that swims close. A dark fish, a rainbow too I think, feeds actively at the head of the run, almost in white water; a beautiful, quiet cutthroat holds a little below me, now dodging an aquatic weed, now taking a nymph.

I have on a minute brassie, about the size of a typed question mark, at the end of twelve feet of fine greased leader. The midge action I am waiting for never happens, but I am lost in watching and don't much care. By moments, I am in the red rainbow's world, nosing the currents. A spin fisherman upstream lands a large brown and throws it back, ceremoniously, observing the law of the river. His kind of fishing, tossing a plug and dragging it back, waiting for a tug, involves the fisherman in the life of the river hardly at all. Careless with his treble hook, it looks as if he's killed the trout he so ostentatiously tossed back, and I grimace as it passes through the run I'm watching, see the red rainbow trail the twitching brown downstream a ways. I holler to the fellow that his fish is dying, that maybe he should net it and take it home, eat it at least. He shouts his answer: he's "already caught it." Such are the Bub Vances of this world.

4. Big Feet

3 August, Dinosaur

The Frémont panels at Cub Creek are well marked on maps of Dinosaur National Monument, and, when we drive up, the broken slope under the rimrock is teeming with children. A van, with the legend "Entertainment for Kids" painted on its side, is parked at the curb. I'm not sure how entertaining they're finding this. Still, kids can make a playground of almost anything. Given the fragility of these sites, perhaps the kids shouldn't be here, too many for a couple of adults to keep track of. Then again, maybe one or two of these children, seemingly inattentive now, goaty on the rocks, maybe one or two of them will register in memory one of the glyphs at Cub Creek and live differently.

Slow lookers, soon enough we have the run of the place. The site proves very extensive, running to the end of the ridge. There are live lizards on the rocks and many large ones pecked into the desert varnish. When a lizard rock-climbs up a sheer face, I see how cunning the lizard glyphs are, at home on the cliffs as a ram or a bison is not. And I find I am again leaning toward the notion that some of the glyphs indicate clan, clan under the sign of the lizard or the bear.

What is unsettling about many of the figures at Cub Creek is the ghostliness of the flesh, which does not appear, except in the occasional stance of eyes or open mouth. The limbs and torso, even the outline of the head, are supplied by the mind. It's only after I looked at several that I noticed this absence. What is pecked into the maroon varnish is ornament—elaborate necklaces and belts, occasional earrings. These are things that must have mattered.

Suddenly, I am again struggling with identity, with how slippery it is, how it shifts, culture to culture, person to person, moment to moment. I am the mercury that runs in a bright rivulet, from face to face, and sometimes just runs.

Beyond the last glyph, the trail bends in a horseshoe around the end of the ridge. There is a good place for sitting there, the view as good as any I have seen. We sit a long time, forgetting what it is to hurry.

4 August, Dry Fork

Perhaps by the time we get to the —V— Ranch in Dry Fork Canyon, I am getting tired, less responsive, having spent the morning at the end of a dusty road, climbing trails and talus slopes at McKee Springs. I am returning; it was here, two years ago, that I first stood before Frémont petroglyphs and staggered. I had happened on the place by chance, dragged away from another day of fishing on the Green by Ellen and my brother, to find myself before these glyphs, bewildered by the unexpectedness of their power, wondering how it could have happened that I had never even heard of the people who had done this, made the walls hum.

The —V— Ranch is private, but Sadie McConkie believed in public access and opened her ranch to the curious. It's still open. But things have changed. The great gateway of deer and elk antlers, an inverted *U*, has been dispersed down a long fence, only six racks left in an arch. There is a shed, a fee on your honor, Cokes in a refrigerator, on your honor, and an array of articles on the ranch's petroglyphs posted on the walls, among them several citing the Royal Panel here as the best rock art on the continent. And the trails have been changed. We'd had a hard time knowing what was trail before; now it's clear, strung wire and hand-lettered signs everywhere. These improvements, well-intentioned, make the glyphs harder to see, much harder.

How lucky we were to have been here before! And, I think, the reading I've been doing about the Frémont and rock art in Utah, as well as the other sites I've seen on this trip west, all get in the way of the glyphs there on the wall. Of course, I do see some things I didn't before: a great shield on a high ledge now accessible by ladder, a hummingbird and a cougar that escaped my notice, and, astoundingly, the heads some of the figures carry in hand, like buckets. I reel—not to have seen what was so obvious! But if I see more, I respond less, and whatever it is I get that I need from petroglyphs is less available to me now. And I miss that owl, riding an arrow, that I can no longer find. Things change: I remember, driving out from Vernal, seeing a gray rabbit on the shoulder of the road—surprised, in a twitch—to see what I had taken for ears take flight, a gray bird that had been perched on a gray stone.

The Royal Panel *is* impressive, the great horned shamans reach out over the valley floor from the cliffs. One of the figures, I notice now, has huge feet, clownish feet. I too have come far on big feet. I walk on to find what for me is the glyph of my travels and the most pedestrian: just two feet connected by a line bent in the shape of a horseshoe, an upside-down *U*. Looking down, I see the *U* that runs up one leg and down the other, connecting my two dusty shoes. We, all of us, just passing through.

5. *Still Out There*

14 August, in camp

It is noon, grasshoppers absorbed in their ardent displays chirring as they rise up over the woodpile, the picnic table, this notepad over which I bend. We are camping up north but still in the Great Basin, on what fly fishermen call the home river. This is the landscape: blue sage, hay-gold grasses, juniper, rabbit-brush, the earth a sandy brown, and in the red rimrock canyon the shining river meandering in a strip of quick green.

Again, this afternoon, I will hike up-canyon from road's end, crossing and recrossing, miles on miles, fishing the blue water, anywhere where there is water enough to show blue in this low-water time. My fly line will whine over the river, quick and green. I don't mind that it doesn't always go where I will it, is subject to quirks and fits. The fishing is easy; I'll hum a little, watch for the rise, wild rainbows coming up for hoppers or caddis flies. We are intent, expressive, finding each other on the barb of our nature.

I remember, fishing far up-canyon, seeing there, where I'd been told, a petroglyph of a fish pecked in the rough basalt of a massive boulder. That trout swims in stone, in the air, a foot or two above high water but under waves of worked stone. And walking out late that night, when I saw the petroglyph, the light, the light thickening in the canyon, finally turning a watered ruby, everything in the canyon manifest, valuable, walking in it all.

My Last Caribou

We got ahead of ourselves first thing. Five minutes from home, before we'd even turned our noses toward Alaska, we were passed by a tire that had got loose of the trailer (the lug nuts, it turned out, had only been thumbed on). We weren't the only ones that tire passed; it was in the fast lane and looked impatient. It was hard to own that tire as ours; it had no place in the day we had imagined. It set us back. In retrospect, that wayward tire seems a fit beginning for our Alaskan safari, at least for mine. It started, I see now, as a comedy of intent, in self-delusion.

The Hunt

The caribou, a lone bull, lay on an open saddle below and two hundred yards down-valley. He was turned a little away from me, at ease, his head low, looking farther down, into the crease. Between where I stood and where he lay, there was a depression, then a rise, then another depression, but there was no cover for a stalk, just ankle-high blueberries. I tested the wind: it was blowing out of the valley.

I weighed my chances. I decided to shoot and got down, slowly, onto the ground, cinching up tight before putting my eye to the scope. Through the scope the bull looked very big, his heavy horns covered in dark velvet, and altogether at ease. He was chewing meditatively, his jaw grinding a methodical circle. He didn't seem to be looking at anything in particular down below, just gazing. An ear twitched, but it didn't turn toward me. I put my thumb on the safety, pushing it down, off. I steadied the crosshairs just behind the bull's shoulder and a few inches down, then settled my breathing, holding the exhalation at the end. With the crosshairs still, I pulled the trigger. The shot sounded oddly muted, a low roar, and then a bounding echo in the distance. The bull stopped chewing; his neck tensed and his ears swung forward, away from me, toward the echo down below. He did not get up. He did not seem particularly disturbed; after a minute he resumed his chewing.

I decided to get closer, and I crouched and crawled my way to the next rise. He was still there, standing now and not far. My second shot staggered him. He did not run. Slowly, he fell, first losing control of his hips then toppling over on his side. I stood up. When I got close, I could hear his rough breathing, but he wasn't moving. When he saw me, he raised one hoof and kicked feebly my way. I stepped close, put the muzzle of my rifle to his neck, and fired. His head went down but then swung back up, the lids of his eyes drawn wide. I fired again. When the echoes stopped, it was very quiet, only my breathing and a little wind. The caribou's eyes no longer looked at me, no longer looked at all.

Across from me the evening sun rolled along the horizon. I could see the bow in it that was the earth's own shape, which the sun would dip below for a short night. At my feet the caribou was still there, not looking as if he were alive. He did not look relaxed but unstrung in a way the living never look: a loss of tension that is the beginning of dissolution.

I did not feel seventeen, a young man finding myself in doing the thing I had imagined, promised in a moment of dead certainty before leaving camp. I felt stupid, stunned, and infinitely abstracted, rapt in the very atmosphere, which was bright and cool and lapping at my temples.

I put up the antenna and called in, wanting, now, to be told what to do. My father thought it too late to get the caribou out before dark. I was to clean it and wait—he'd be there at first light with our homemade gurney.

In the diminished light I considered how to make the long cut from sternum to pelvis. The side hill was steep enough and the bull heavy enough that the cut was not easy. I made it by propping the upper rear leg on my head, and then the hot entrails slid out with a rush, flowing in a lumpy mass around my boots. That done, I found a rock to wait out the night on. I thought of the grizzlies that were rumored to have come right into camp before we arrived and torn a caribou carcass from where it cured in a tree. They were said to come up out of the valleys at night, on a breeze. I gazed down-valley, but even in the half-light of the Alaskan white nights I could see little more than what I imagined.

Photo: The Trophy
In this picture, I am kneeling with the bull's horns propped on one knee, my face, with its young man's first beard, not smiling, framed between the sweeping palms. It's a photograph of a traditional pose, not of me nor of that caribou who looked toward an echo when he should have looked back, toward a prone figure with its gun.

It was a puzzled boy who sat on that rock, with blood on his boots and his hands and the moon on his shoulder. "Cleaning" the caribou had not been clean; it had been butchery, and butchery badly done. Although I knew better, I had slit the bladder and then had a hard time getting the windpipe cut. The caribou's slack tongue lolled obscenely when I pulled on the windpipe with my left hand, sawing away with the knife in my right. There was no one there to pound my back or tell me how to understand what I had done or how to do what I needed to do. I have not forgotten the mess. When it comes to mind, I know I'm the one who made it, who shot the caribou that couldn't place me, did not run, who *gutted it out* in the long Alaskan twilight.

At School

I would remember all this years later, fretting one night over the Middle English text of *Sir Gawain and the Green Knight*. I remembered about halfway through what seemed an absurdly long and joyful account of butchering "dos" and other "dere," the spoils of a single day in the field. The text is seamless, a long celebration. If the hunters felt no pity, they were not confused. Their hunt was prescribed in manuals, like Edward Duke of York's *The Master of Game*. Then the hunt was an art and butchering the deer was art too; the author loved to describe the hunters' great proficiency at it in a language as precise as their carving. From the first cut to feeding the hounds their bloody meal, the deer were butchered according to book; even the bit thrown into the bush, the "raven's fee," was rote.

The hunt and the carving were all venery. *Venery*. The word makes me uneasy, though why it should is hard to say. There's a wound there that hasn't healed. The venom is still pulsing, from the boy on his rock to the man who sits here, writing. *Venery*, two words, really, but close, twins in the language. One calls up the world of the hunt; the other the world of the bedroom. Venison and Venus. The root notion is desire, for wild game, for the other to be there. Etymologically, the two pursuits diverged; each had its own word, only by chance finding in English the same form. Perhaps not entirely by chance. The link is in our literature, certainly in *Gawain*, where Gawain's temptations in

bed (back at the castle) are cannily juxtaposed with the Green
Knight's exploits in the field.

In Town

The day we went to meet the plane in Anchorage, my brother
wasn't on it. The passengers trailed out along the pavement,
then the crew, but no Keith. There had been heavy weather in
Alaska that week, floods, and Keith had thought it unlikely we
had made it to the rendezvous. On the phone it was decided that
he would fill an empty seat the next day, and we would camp
over. We went sightseeing, tourists for a day rather than hunters.
We looked at what was left to see of the big earthquake of 1964,
when expectations about how the world would act proved dead
wrong (the harbor emptying into a valley in minutes). But resi-
dents seemed to think that since it was an Alaskan quake, it
ought to have been big. Alaska sold big: hamburgers the size of
salad plates and the world's biggest stuffed bears at the local museum. Kodiak, polar, grizzly—they were bigger than I had been
able to imagine during my vigil on the rock.

Restless, I decided my brother could arrive without me, that I
needed to rub against some teenagers. It was 1967, the "summer
of love," a hard summer to be a teenager so far from San Fran-
cisco. I went to a dance. There was a sort of dancing going on
there, a stumbling, self-conscious version of what they must
have thought was being done elsewhere. The locals seemed to
have the comical idea that I, from *Oregon*, could speak for our
generation, must know. I claimed ignorance, *was* ignorant, but
they did not believe me, took me for coy.

I am sorry to have missed my brother's first steps in Alaska,
not because the dance proved grotesque but because his entrance translated immediately into the family chronicles, and I
would like to have seen the event. Phobic about flying, especially
flying in bad weather, Keith started drinking hours before

boarding the plane and kept it up. The liquid nerve was good enough to get him there, but his first act in Alaska was to spew the lot on the tarmac. In answer to my mother's startled exclamation, he coolly observed he had "puked in better places." If I had been there, perhaps I would have thought to ask what places.

Photo: Brothers in Arms
In this picture I stand with my brother, two hunters with rifles. It's August but cold; we're dressed for it, in gloves, my brother all in black, and there I am, all khaki above the jeans. We are wearing floppy hats from Goodwill. We look as if we believe in our pose; perhaps we did. I carried this photo in my wallet for over twenty years. So much of being brothers, friends, is shared delusion.

On Mount Fairplay

At the road, my father and I agreed to meet at the summit of Mount Fairplay. He would go up the left side of the ridge where we stood, I the right. Keith, who had driven the truck one more mile and parked it, would come up another slope, meeting us on top.

The mountain had its own sound: the sound of water running, out of sight, beneath the stones. The slope I climbed was porous, combed with invisible rills. It was a long hike to the top; the tricks of distance had fooled us again. The summit proved not to be a point but a small plateau. White, shed antlers of caribou littered the ground, some gnawed by porcupines but most intact, with their distinctive shovels and palms. I wandered among bones, consciousness broken by points of light, on the edge of migraine or blackout. I stopped, looking over the toes of my boots six feet down into a blue pool, there, at the bottom of a

pocket on the mountaintop. The water had the opacity of a blue
eye, and tumbled down in it were caribou horns, white out of the
water and a parrot green in it. I looked up, feeling a stick figure
under an immense sky.

Keith and my father never did show on the summit of Mount
Fairplay. From the rim of the plateau I finally spotted them, in
the truck, driving slowly away. I looked through my scope: there
could be no doubt. Rage rolled through my veins. I bellowed
something less than words into the cool air, firing my rifle again
and again into the indifferent sky.

My father, on a different slope of Mount Fairplay, had suffered a loss of perspective of his own. He had seen, on the
heights above him, a brown animal, climbing with the ambling
gait of a bear. It had been moving off, going away from him. My
father, with a bear tag in his pocket, had begun a stalk, hoping to
get close enough for a shot. He had spent a long time at it before
he found that his quarry was not a bear in the distance but a porcupine not so far away.

Recently, camping out in the wilds of Pennsylvania, I tried to explain to a friend how my father could have mistaken that porcupine for a bear. I talked about the tricks of distance and the family resemblance of porcupine and bear; it came out a comic
story, my father a figure of fun, which was not what I intended. I
thought it was a story about perspective and perception. But
even as I spoke, my father's vindication was ambling through
camp. A stirring at the margin of the lantern light proved to be
the creature in question. He looked, his brown eyes bright in the
weak light, then turned and wandered away. We were still
chuckling over this slim chance when a hubbub broke out at the
next camp. In the light of their campfire we could see startled
men jumping up and heard one frightened voice call out "bear."

If I were writing fiction, I would leave this bit out as unbeliev-
able, but I'm not; it happened. So much that happens does not

have the appearance of truth. That porcupine came back four times during the night, to gnaw at the logs of the campground lean-to we were trying to sleep in. Three times I, a gawky figure in shorts, chased him into the woods, suggesting more emphatically each time that he stay in the woods. Finally, I dislodged what must have been to him a very attractive log, replacing it with a stray masonry block. The porcupine came back, and I heard in the silence a single stroke of tooth on concrete, and then he was gone.

I have had a letter from my father. I asked him to write, to recount what he remembered about my last caribou and the hike up Mount Fairplay. He remembers that I was angry that there was no one to meet me on the summit of Fairplay. I can tell he regrets not getting to the top, and I am ashamed that I have let him regret such a small thing for so many years. It was no more than a missed appointment. What happened on Mount Fairplay did not admit of a father, of any other. I felt betrayed and thought it was by my father, and I *was* betrayed—betrayed by a story. The story told me that to hunt alone, to make the kill, made a man and would resolve the confusions of being seventeen. On Mount Fairplay I took the small disappointment for the big one.

About my caribou hunt, in one particular my father's story veers disturbingly far from the one I've told here. He remembers, as my mother does, that though delayed by tire trouble, they spotted my flashlight about ten that night and were able to reach me soon thereafter. He says we loaded the field-dressed caribou on our gurney and struggled with that load until nearly two, when we gave out, skinned the caribou, and left it where it was. He remembers that we returned early the next morning and were relieved to find the caribou had not been discovered by bears but had only been pecked a little by birds (the ravens had their fee!).

Photo: The Author's Mother
This is a picture of my mother, carrying
the caribou horns. They are tied to a
packboard that is strapped to her back,
the shovels below her waist and the
palms arcing over her head. She has on
an orange hat, like a hunter, and is carrying a small rifle over her right shoulder. She stands in the stance of a sol-
dier ready to march, but my mother is
smiling. Does she smile because she's
uneasy in that get-up or because the
camera demands it or to acknowledge
that, though she packed the horns out,
the picture tells a lie? She is not a
hunter. She is along.

And so, without intending it, I have revised the hunt in memory, stretching an hour or two of waiting into a night on a rock.
But perhaps the hunt I remember is the better story, better rep-
resents the "truth" of my experience   that transformation requires a dark passage. If I did not greet the new day a man, I was
not the same boy either. I owned my actions, and I discovered
that the hunter's formula was not mine, that hunting required a
presumption about man's place I did not share. If man looked
suddenly small in the landscape, the landscape itself was alive,
teemed with consciousness and desire. Until I intruded on that
world with a gun, I had not been able to feel the singing
sufficiency of the bird's life, the coyote's world alive with coyote
energy.

Like my shot into the valley, the effects of that hunt have echoed
through the twenty-one years I have waited to write. I had re-
minders. The caribou horns found their resting place in the
garage back home. In the years they hung there, the once fine
velvet sheath dried and split, began to peel, revealing white
bone. They had been a part of the caribou's dignity, impressive

in their large, slow sweep when he turned his head to look down-valley. When I came home from dates, they were the last thing I saw on Friday and Saturday nights when I pulled the car into the garage and turned out the lights. They never quite disappeared into the wall; they never got that familiar.

On Mount Fairplay I still carried a gun, but soon thereafter I gave my rifle away. I could no longer imagine an occasion when I would have a use for it. I fell out of love with Hemingway. I found more to admire in Japan's holy fools, like Ryōkan, who cut a square from the roof of his hut, Gogō-an, so that the bamboo shoot that had found a way through his floor could grow on, unimpeded; or like Issa, whose compassion extended even to bugs, to the fleas and lice that were his companions when he journeyed, and to the flies of his home:

> I'm going out now,
> So enjoy yourselves making love,
> Flies of my hut!

Although I have renounced the hunt, I tell the story of my last caribou often. I have moved often, and in making new friends, have answered the implicit question "who are you?" with the stories that tell my life. I do not tell this story for effect but find myself telling it, whatever the effect. I have not found that we get to choose our stories; maybe actors do or people who act their lives. I speak; I have not often asked why. The story resists interpretation, the text is too familiar, coated with retellings. I went to Alaska to hunt, wanting the hunter's rite, to come back simplified, a man. I came back stunned, like Coleridge's "ancyent marinere," who shot the harmless albatross, and was compelled, by "that anguish" that came according to periods he did not understand, to begin his tale again and again. The story isn't *for* the mariner; it *is* the mariner. If the story has a *for*, it's for the wedding guest, and it keeps him from the gladness of the wedding and the feast. Perhaps, like the medieval hunters in

Gawain, I hunted according to the book, only thinking the book was Hemingway.

Where we crossed out of the Yukon into Alaska, the road changed from gravel to blacktop. After a thousand miles of dust, I got down on my knees and kissed the pavement—I thought the rest of the way would be smooth going. It hasn't been.

A Coleridge Walk

Preamble

Perhaps Dion did sing his "Wanderer" from our car's small speaker, once, when the family joke about Grandpa's "straightening out the road" got told again. I remember it that way. Or perhaps the lyrics were just going round in my head. Either way, the song and the joke live together in memory.

The joke wasn't funny, exactly; any laughter it elicited was nervous laughter. Even then Grandpa was old, and we all thought his constant fudging on the center line, on the bent country roads of Oregon, was going to get him into trouble—that there would be a crash or a ticket and hell to pay. He finally did get into some trouble with his driving, but not straightening out the road. It is memory that jogs me here, and memory is bent, a wanderer on curvy roads (never as straight as the imagined future is).

I suppose that, for my grandfather, straightening out the road was a good thing, made sense, the shortest distance and all that. Straightness, we're led to believe, is good, a virtue (and manly). Grandpa spoke out of our culture's mainstream, the straightest part of any stream. In school, stiff teachers, to form you, spoke the brittle formulas: "Sit up straight!" "Straighten up!" "Get this straight!" "Let me straighten you out!" Such phrases convey—

don't I hear it?—a veiled "or else." Not "or else you will be bent" but a chuck or a clout. Straightness, apparently, does not call to children. They don't come to it out of love but from fear of flogging.

They cut down the glen to build the grade school I attended, Glenfair, and laid out in its place great squares of grass and pavement, rectangular football fields, diamonds for baseball. Inside, bad boys—the bent, the warped, the twisted boys, who would not heed a warning—were disciplined with a straightedge, a ruler, for raps on a boy's crook fingers, or a yardstick, for swats. Beyond the geometry of the school grounds, in open fields cut to stubble, footpaths marked the boy's way home. That way was not straight but coursed serpentine. There, dizzy whistling was permitted.

An Amble with S. T. C.

One morning in the winter of 1798, midwinter but fine, another boy, William Hazlitt, accompanied the poet Coleridge "six miles on the road." They talked while walking. It was a tramp Hazlitt would remember, and I remember it too, having read Hazlitt: "I observed that he continually crossed me on the way by shifting from one side of the footpath to the other. This struck me as an odd movement; but I did not at that time connect it with any instability of purpose or involuntary change of principle, as I have done since. He seemed unable to keep a straight line." It's a comical picture: the bemused Hazlitt bumped into the bracken by the wandering, expostulating poet. Coleridge seemed to "float in the air" as he passed from "subject to subject," shifting side to side on the path. But as portrait, this passage is not only comical; it's also damning. The Coleridge walk offends Hazlitt's sense of rectitude. Not keeping the straight way, finally, is seen as a moral failing, a failure of will. Yet isn't it Coleridge's very meandering that Hazlitt remembers, and that holds us after two hundred years?

It seems to me good, if a different order of good from "good boys," that the figure of the meander should take its name from a river, a particular river in Asia Minor that the Greeks called *Maiandros*. It is, of course, a river in bends. But it is a river, fluent and material, irregular and changing, and it is there, cool to the dipped foot. Few abstractions remember their whence so well.

They tell us that water, left alone, takes the path of least resistance, down. The shortest distance does not figure or is only a figure in the mind. Running water cuts the earth on the outside bend, accretes on the inside, and meanders more. The bends widen, and the water runs deepest where it cuts. In open country such a stream is slow-moving and seems to get nowhere. And we want even a stream to get somewhere, soon, wherever it's going, and soon means straightly ("go straight home").

I floated the meanders once, in a life raft, all day. At the end of that day, when I had clambered out and pulled the raft up the bank, I was dumbfounded to see the car I'd left that morning only three hundred yards away, across a cow field. As I gaped, one of the cows lowed, switched its tail (bugs). Disappointment followed my surprise: I hadn't gotten anywhere! Only later did I find in that day one of the days I remember. Low down in a life raft, going round in an eddy, I rode the waters of Lethe, forgetting not the past but the future, where the water we imagine runs straight, like water in a ditch or a canal.

Blind Staggers

Often, of course, we *fall under* the spell of clarity. An idea well stated is so much less messy than a thing, than something happening. Perhaps we prefer it out of squeamishness; perhaps we're just entranced by its regular lines. The future seems straight to us because it hasn't happened. So the straightness of our imagined time, its linear tidiness, takes its place there.

"That was weird" is the head-shaking response to what happens. I hear it often, more often all the time. Perhaps it means no more than what has happened was unexpected, not what we imagined, not straight. At root, *weird* means to turn, to wind, and it came to mean fate, destiny, "that which befalls" us. This etymology is in itself weird, that is, must seem weird to us. What once meant *that which happens* now means *to seem strange*. Have straightened expectations estranged us from the event, from accepting what befalls us? To accept things bent is to accede to them, not to order ("straighten up there!") but to ask—"tell us, tell us,"—and bending close hear earth answer, "*tellus.*"

The better life we imagine is over there, straight down the middle of a fairway. In heading that way we head away from circumstance, the great surround. Looking to the future we say we see it ahead, on the horizon, but the real horizon is round, circumscribes us.

Do we accept less of curvaceous fate than Coleridge? Less yet than the man who said, not sang drunk in words not much understood, *wuld lung syne?* Or the one before him who said *ald* and *wyrd* to name his sense of the shape of life's twists? Is our ancestor "meanderthal"? Perhaps, but that impulse, to trace a *line* of descent, is itself an attempt to "think straight" about origin.

Aborigines, whom we imagine somehow behind us in time, though they are as now as we are, are said to "go walkabout." It's a phrase gone sour. It did mean just that going about, that gathering of food, that had so little to do with supermarkets. It was part, too, of a young aborigine's initiation—*to be able* to walk about, go it alone. Perhaps it still means these things. But from the straight perspectives of city streets, it's now more often a synonym for malingering. "Gone walkabout" is "gone native," to have fallen from the great white way, from single-mindedness. Sometimes walkabout just means gone on a drunk. So it goes: out of the dreamtime into the great exchanges where men "trade futures."

Go Back On

1.

It's a wet place. Last time I was there, it drizzled, most other times too; but I go back, "keep going back" (that *keep* puzzles me, as if the going back were possessed). All that's left is a stretch of hummocky grass with an asphalt turnout in the shape of a keyhole, left of man's doing, that is: the creek still rushes through a last elbow out onto the sand, and the ocean is there, up near the grass at high tide. When it's out, there are rocks and tide pools. The place is bound in by Strawberry Hill on one end and a rock promontory at the other (where the cave is). The sign that now names the place says "Bob Creek." It's a sign put there by the state of Oregon; the one before it said "Purdy's" and was probably put up by someone named Purdy (that possessive referred to a bent row of cabins, "for let").

My family "took" one for a week in the fifties. In those days I was clumsy and most admired by my mother for my ability to fall gracefully, which meant falling loose-limbed and not getting hurt. I fell in the creek, several times, and in other places less slippery. My feet were big and often pointed to as probable cause. No one, I think, quite believed the explanation, not me anyway. I never felt the need of an excuse; I was proud to be good at falling (so much that's good is fallen into).

That first trip was vacation. I hardly remember it. I was traveling beyond the pale, in a world I had few words for. In place of memory there is a feeling of weight, volume, all inarticulate. Sometimes traveling now, I find again that nameless world, the true exotic, and stutter. Sometimes I find it traveling in the backyard. We're not encouraged to look; professional travelers write for the most part a glib prose, as if the exotic was for them foreknown—not exotic, only "colorful."

I do remember having run over a black sand speckled with white chips, and at dusk swinging a stone on the end of a leather thong, in whirring circles, to bring a bat down; the smell of dead fish, the mewing of the gulls on Strawberry Hill. But these memories are extrinsic, hang on, for life, to the sense of what I can't remember (as translucent sea lice cling to blueback, the *harvest* trout, in those rivers).

2.

It was bulldozers brought Purdy's down, and a thorough job they did of it: nothing remains, no foundation, no sign at all. What was imagined—imagined by rote if the evidence of the coast is fair—was revised, again by rote, along modernist lines. Only the colloquial tone of the name endured: "Purdy's" to "Bob Creek." So someone bulldozed the bent cabins at Purdy's, "straightened things out." But that was not the first cleaning up at Bob Creek in historical time ("our" history). It was the logging before that. There's a little first-growth here and there (at Cape Perpetua!) to remind us of that primeval "before." Then, when the crews laid down the roadbeds for Highway 101, they bulldozed the Indian shell mounds all up and down the coast, at Bob Creek too, paving over the too obvious signs of a human before.

Thoreau, at his cabin, saw a chance in the language to pry his readers from the spell of reading, to characterize the way they lived as trance. I'm thinking, you know, of his toying with the Anglicism "sleepers," the ties in the roadbed of the railway. "Each one is a man" in the sleep of work or pleasure: "They are sound sleepers." Thoreau hoped they might "sometime get up again," and perhaps they did, so soon did the sleepers of his roadbeds become the bulldozers of ours. But if they got up, they did not wake up but got up as zombies, active, charged with intent. Is it a tale "full of soul" that ends in a metamorphosis into caterpillars?

Still, the job got done; another trip, passing by, I saw through the rear window (and the nausea of a curvy road) the machinations of the "earth movers." That year we drove by.

3.

What is peculiar about the way I remember my trips to (and at) Bob Creek is that I remember them together. They constellate. The place speaks in the association of experiences there, more than in the experiences themselves (as constellations in a night sky are not the stars but the relations we see among them). At home, what happens falls into place, fits too neatly into how I think, conforms. Traveling eccentrically, not going back, is narrative—"and then." I remember it as story. And these are shapes of experience we're encouraged in (it's bias, not accident, that, at root, *narrative* means knowing, and *story*, wisdom).

As a visitor, then, just a looker, I go back, traveling light. I'm empty, on vacation from my possessions (an asceticism of travel, the food is mortification).

4.

At the end of the long beach, at the open mouth of the cave, I sniff and pause, something foul in there. But I go in, stumbling over the worn stones. Urine smell, but something else too, rank. In the gloom I see what it is: a great log has washed in on a high tide and stuck there, and in the wet and dark sprouted like a potato in a drawer.

The log is old, worn smooth in the surf and bleached by the sun, dead but sending out thousands of shoots—white, sticky ribbons, some three feet long. I take a long look, touch, smell enough to remember (*pay* attention; in our language it's an economy of loss).

5.

Another year the cave is sea-scrubbed, the tide high enough to roar as I scramble in. I watch my step; these tumbled stones are slick. Two I find are smooth, black, featureless. Shaped like brains, I think, without the fissure of a thought, and cool. Holding them quiets me, quiets the perpetual yakking. I press one, then the other, to my forehead, my temples, and emerge into the light (cool *is* light). I carry them the long walk back up the beach, heavy, one in each hand, balanced up high like breasts.

6.

Another time, I see that the black sand of the beach at Bob Creek is ground stone; the white chips, ground shells, fallen from the Indian shell mounds in the face of the eroding cliffs (what is left that the bulldozers didn't get). I cross Bob Creek on the highway bridge, wade out to the mouth through the weedy flats, to where the seam of buried shells lies in its thick bed. I read: the charcoal of cook fires, what they ate: mussels, limpets, clams, snails, abalone and fish, deer bones, a rib, bones I can't identify. It's a midden, garbage, evidence (what's left to see, not story). I spot a thin ring in the bank, which I pull at: it arcs out, a great tooth, a fang, bear.

7.

What happened at Bob Creek, then, constellates, and its form moves me. So at the Oregon Historical Society, I struggle with the short story, the white story of the Indians in the area. The accounts are sketchy at best. Even the tribal boundaries are inconsistently drawn; the Siuslaw or the Lower Umpqua, probably the Lower Umpqua, lived at Bob Creek. In 1840, Jason Lee put in at such a village—the hope was for a mission. In his story the Lower Umpqua were "miserable fish-eaters at the mouth of the river, who were as savage as the bears, their neighbors"—*their neighbors*! Then the Umpqua *confirmed* a faith, an ethos; now dead, they erode another. I welcome them.

I read, too, how sometimes the spirit of the dead—and there were so many dead in the last years—could not quite get free of the body but reentered it, grew hair all over, and took refuge in the hills of the coast range. If hunters, out after deer or elk, smelled in the wind something horrible, they knew such a thing was about, and they knew how to escape it.

What they called Bob Creek, this stretch of beach and the stream itself, I can't find; but Cape Perpetua was "the red ochre place" (not so perpetual), where they quarried red face paint; Cook's Chasm, nearby, was "where the penis goes in," and it was there they dug for the blues of their body paint. But for Bob Creek, no name, just the sense that it had another name, before, and that it feels like a name I can't remember: it has insensible weight. I fall out of Bob Creek, out of Purdy's. The gulls hang down from gray cloud; I depend on them.

✿ ✿ ✿

A Tail

Three days ago I went back. A new sign specifically forbids picking at the cliff face (though it does not mention shell mounds or the Umpqua, the "spirit" of archaeological preservation probably put the sign there). For the first time I see someone else investigating the seams of shells over by the stream (signs are good for that; they point). I go over with my hands in my pockets but stoop to retrieve from the loose debris at creek's edge three shells. They are beautiful, wonderfully formed in the shape of moths or butterflies, the bodies dark olive, the wings a bleached pink.

They're on my desk now. I think, look at them, and think again. These memories want each other—I hold to that, though I hear causality whisper its favorite word: coincidence. I hope to reform that word, remember that it means only "happens together"; the pejorative echo need not follow. It's curious how the habit of causality intrudes, again and again, to belittle what feels like significant relation with that word *coincidence*, curious too that a mind set on finding causes should so often find cause to use a word that denies cause. It stops me, sometimes; sometimes I go back on it.

Dr. Williams's Medicine Bundle

1. The Old Camp Hole

At night the way down could be difficult. By lantern light our trail and the many game trails looked all alike. Often we were all on one trail. A boy then, I waited while the men up front bent over the intersections, deciding. From the tail of our small company, I watched as we snaked ahead in the darkness, a procession of lights, bright legs lit below, dark manshapes looming above.

Sometimes mistakes were made and acknowledged by swinging a lantern over the darkness that was precipice, the rush of water rising out of the canyon below. Sometimes we were lost, had to backtrack, but we always made it, scrambling through brush the last bit to the river's edge and camp. The Deschutes ran black in the night, a web of starlight just visible on its glassy skin. Someone always shone a flashlight into the river, to gauge its height and the clarity of the water, guessing if the fishing would be good or hard going. Awake in my sleeping bag, I watched the stars' progress in their watery darkness, pulsing, between cliffs of live stone. Then it was morning, our smoke twisting up between the ruddy walls of the canyon, the sizzle of camp cooking, my small body remembering hunger.

The canyon turns back on itself at the foot of the camp hole, where Squaw Creek joins the Deschutes. The trail there is over a stone outcrop. At its base, on the upstream side of it, there is a sandy cave. I crawled in there many times, slept there once, always wondering if it had been shelter for the Indians that Squaw Creek was named for. Running my fingers through the cool sand, I found shells of freshwater clams, nothing else. Atop the outcrop, I sat by a U.S. Geological Survey benchmark, a dark brass disk, and gazed cross river at the creek's canyon. It was out of reach, the river too dangerous for a child to wade, and it was closed to all fishing, a sanctuary for spawning steelhead. Still, I wanted to walk in that canyon.

Every year I was less of a fisherman—lucky, but attention wandering. I would catch fish while loafing on my back on a boulder midstream, casting over my head into the river's glassy currents. Once I was playing a small trout that way, not bothering to look around, when my rod tip pulled down, heavy. I stood up and in the deep green watched a snaky Dolly Varden thrash its head side to side, my trout a bright sliver of moon in its dark mouth. I was lucky. But I wanted something else. Back at my schoolboy's desk in midwinter, I sketched the stream, trying with a pencil to get back, to be in sage and juniper, in an arid landscape cut by the river in its canyon. I wanted to carry that place in me when I was away, in the city. I began to dream at my desk, stuttering when called on, estranged.

I stopped fishing but kept going back. It was only in the early days of my going that we packed into the camp hole, actually camped there. Perhaps the fathers, getting older, had begun to feel the weight of the packs. When I went there later, without them, the habit was lost, and I always camped on the canyon rim, where the stars rode clear down to the low horizon. Then night was for talking, banked sagebrush fires, day for hiking in the canyon or on the great stone headlands. By then I had realized that, whatever else I was doing, I was always looking for an arrowhead, something for my pocket, something to keep the place alive in memory when I was away. But I never found one in the canyon.

2. Rattlers and Bull

By all reports, the canyon up and down from the camp hole was snaky. We boys were instructed to keep an eye peeled, to watch where we put our feet and our hands; we were told what to do if we were bitten, then let go on our own. The warnings were matter-of-fact, and I hoped more than feared that I would meet up with a rattlesnake; for years I saw snakes in twisted sticks and heard them in the chirr of insects. The snakes kept me alert, alive in my senses. They were good for that. Many times I met startled fisherman, coming downstream or climbing out of the canyon, who had just seen a rattler, two holes upstream—there, under that juniper, on the trail down by Huddle Rock (the spot was usually pointed to with a rod tip).

Getting along the river could be tough. Open away from water, the canyon was brushy close to it. Sometimes getting to streamside meant crawling down a sandy chute and wading through a patch of nettles. The best fishing hole on the river was a place like that, and as long as I fished I was willing to crawl to it. One time I emerged from the brush to see young Jimmy shivering in his shorts next to a fire that was more smoke than flame. His wet clothes hung in the bushes next to the fire, and Jimmy was doing a chattering little dance to keep from freezing. The river's edge is slippery there; a spring seeps from a seam in the overhanging ledge, and in the perpetual shadow the rocks are covered with an ocher slime. I had worried about falling in there, because the river is deep, deeper than my pole would reach, and fast, filled with bubbles to the bottom. But Jimmy hadn't slipped, his father had pushed him in at the sudden whir of rattlesnake. Then, in a frenzy, he let the snake get away, first trying to swat it with his pole (and catching a tree), then swinging a stick that proved too rotten to make much of a club. Sometime thereafter he fished Jimmy out of the river and lit the smudge. I never saw that snake; I never met a rattlesnake in the canyon.

Bull snakes are another matter. Just downstream from where Jimmy went swimming, the river spreads into a green pool. Once we got old Thompson down into the canyon, down the chute, to that very pool. He saw the big rock that juts into the water there as an inviting place for a nap, and we left him to it. He was joined, while he slept there in the sun, by a bull snake. It curled up under the pack he was using for a pillow and gave him quite a start when he found it. He was laughing when I got back but had already decided he was never coming back. Bull snakes look a lot like rattlesnakes; they don't have a wedge-shaped head or rattles, of course, but the pattern on their backs is close enough to cause confusion, particularly just waking up.

Another time, packing out, on the stone outcrop below the camp hole, my father reached past me on the narrow trail and grabbed at a diamondback I hadn't seen, was about to step on. He swung it into the air like a whip, once around overhead, and slammed it down against the rock face below the trail. Adrenaline is a wonderful thing. But that turned out to be a bull snake, too, and soon enough we were sorry it was dead.

3. Medicine

William Carlos Williams, a doctor who made house calls, carried the black bag of his trade when he was about his trade. It was probably on the seat next to him in a moment, which he records in "To Elsie," in lines that seem to suggest the felt oppressiveness of not seeing what is there:

> the imagination strains
> after deer
> going by fields of goldenrod in
>
> the stifling heat of September

In "To Elsie," the world seems available only in "isolate flecks." And yet, looking for deer, perhaps Williams didn't so much lose sight of the goldenrod as find it obliquely. Not seeing deer is an occasion, too, and the mind awakens to the world in absence as well as in presence. To look for is not to see what we imagine but to attend to what is there by seeing what it's not. The goldenrod is there, in the poem, and if it is not as radiant as the "isolate flecks" Williams celebrates, it is there more constantly, a presence gathering on the rim of absence. The world sometimes comes close in seeing, sometimes it answers. George Oppen whispers in "Psalm":

> The wild deer bedding down—
> That they are there!

And we know their being there is enough, because it is everything.

Sometimes when we look we find. Emerson records of Thoreau that "those pieces of luck which happen only to good players happened to him. One day, walking with a stranger, who inquired where Indian arrowheads could be found, he replied, 'Everywhere,' and, stooping forward picked one on the instant from the ground." It doesn't often happen that way. In *Paterson*, Williams's Dr. P., walking in the park,

> leans, in his stride,
> at sight of a flint arrow-head
> (it is not)
> —there
> in the distance, to the north, appear
> to him the chronic hills

It is no small thing to be given the hills, and looking for arrowheads and snakes along the Deschutes, I found the canyon. The river that runs there runs here too, though I write this three thousand miles away.

Even if Dr. P. found no arrowhead on his walk in the park, William Carlos Williams had picked arrowheads from the plowed fields of Virginia. He gave one to his alter ego, Dev Evans, to carry in his pocket on his *Voyage to Pagany*. I imagine Williams carried one, too. I like to think of it as a kind of medicine bundle, medicine for a man in cities too much. An arrowhead is something from the old people, appropriate for a medicine bundle. An arrowhead has the human on it, is healing. It remembers a way of being in, not against, the world.

4. Squaw Creek

When dams on the Deschutes put an end to steelhead spawning in Squaw Creek, the Oregon State Fish and Game Commission, acknowledging that there were no longer any steelhead taking sanctuary there, opened it to trout fishing at last. The news reawakened my childhood desire to explore Squaw Creek's canyon, and a trip was planned.

I had recently read Craig Lesley's first novel about the Nez Perce Dreamers and talking to him, had gotten a recommendation for a restaurant that served Indian fry bread (our high brows were riding rather low that night). It just happened to be on the way to Squaw Creek, on the Warm Springs Indian Reservation, right where Highway 26 crosses the Deschutes. The place was in the same spot as the diner we had stopped at on the way to the camp hole years before (the talismanic food then had been a stale maple bar). I ordered the fry bread. We all did. And it was good. I followed my considerably rounded belly out the door and down the twisted dirt roads and many turnings that led on to Squaw Creek.

The last turn was over a rocky shoulder and down to where the two-track road ran into the creek. We didn't ford but pulled into the tall cheat grass. With the engine off, the bugs in the canyon resumed their conversation, and we joined in, comparing rocky places where we might be able to get a tent stake in.

But as soon as I stirred from the car, the coiling and uncoiling in my abdomen reminded me that the "fry" in fry bread means fried. I was hearing the call, nay the shout, of nature. We were in open country, low sage and small juniper; the situation did not look promising. I struck out on a game trail for the rimrock up-canyon. I remember thinking, as I climbed: Call of nature! What a culture, so damn citified it's reduced nature to a bowel move-ment. By the time I was over the first rise, my stride was consid-erably impaired, but I had about decided that I didn't mind "the call of nature," that I liked being reminded that nature starts so close. When I clambered over the rock rim of the canyon, I could wait to answer no more. Huddling in the sage, I gazed cross canyon, at first blankly but then attentively, my eyes focus-ing on the dark mouth of a cave. It looked interesting, and I fixed its location in mind before strolling down to make camp.

We were hardly out of sight of the car the next morning when we found a small rattler in the hollow of a pine stump. It wasn't as big around as a child's pencil and had only a button for a rattle, but it was a rattlesnake. We had a good look at it, then headed upstream, my wife, Ellen, out front, frisky in the cold air. Tom, Keith, and I trailed after her, a concert of yawns. The canyon narrowed, opened, and narrowed again. Ponderosa pine grew tall in the slot; Squaw Creek rushed in its rocky chute. Red and yellow lichen painted the sheer cliffs overhead. We crossed the creek on stepping-stones, then headed back down toward breakfast. Keith took the lead on a heavily traveled deer trail that ran along a steep slope over the creek. The sun was bright on the other side of the canyon, but in the shade our breaths still steamed. When Keith hissed "snake," our eight-legged animal came to a sudden halt. Just ahead an enormous rattlesnake lay coiled on the trail. It wasn't moving, and Keith said what I was thinking, "Looks like a cow chip." We began to wonder if the snake might be dead, so Keith prodded it a little with a longish stick, finally tipping it on its side. To our surprise, the tipped snake got its balance and rolled down the sidehill like a bike tire, finally bumping to a stop fifteen or twenty yards below us. There, it came to life, rattling, angry. Soon there was nothing to be seen of it but the serpentine track it left in the sand.

When I thought we were even with the cave, I cut up the side of the canyon, while the others headed down, for camp. I picked my way slowly on the steep slope, looking for a cave at the foot of the cliff face. Before I had gone far, I saw smoke from camp and heard the sounds of cooking mingling with the murmur of voices. The roof of the cave was blackened by fires kindled by other hands. I sat down on a block of stone inside the mouth of the cave. It was the best seat; many must have sat there before me, huddling close to a fire or getting out of rough weather. Some of them must have brought their paints, because red figures were scattered here and there on the live stone of the ceiling and the cave walls. There was an abstract design that appeared often, red bands, some connected, some broken, all drawn in the shape of an oval. But the figures that arrested my attention were people. A human figure walking toward me, with another, like the first one but smaller, walking behind, and after them, faded but distinct enough to see, someone on a small horse. I turned my head toward the mouth of the cave, the way they were looking, looking too. Things came close: the cool air stood in the canyon, bright, watery, the wind a slow wave rolling over the creek and up to the mouth of the cave. Blooming sage. Swaying trees, tall grasses. Crow talking. I sat with my "antlered thoughts," listened and watched. Finally, I called out, sure my friends would want to wait on breakfast.

Later that day I hiked down to the old camp hole with Keith and Ellen. We looked across the river to the campsites, hollowed out in the brush and trees, abandoned now. There was no boy over there. It was the same place, but it was out of reach. We were on the other side of the river now. We soon turned back, hiking the game trails up-canyon. We chattered as we went, and our voices sounded in my ears no different than the chattering of blue jays or camp robbers.

Coda

Sometimes, dreaming at my desk, I find myself back at the mouth of the cave above Squaw Creek. I see a girl in there, a wild child. She's wearing a baseball cap, something she carried away from her home in the city. There's a small bow and a quiver of arrows, sticks for a fire, and a box of Blue Diamond matches. She doesn't see me, she's drawing something on the wall of the cave. She's painting with lipstick, and the stone under her hand has her whole attention.

Kinds of Motion

> *"Does he like rocks?"*
> *"He loves rocks," Diana said.*
> *"Then tell him, from me, Tafraoute."*

1.

Agadir, Tiznit, eight hours on a slow bus. Then two hours more to Tafraoute on a single lane of blacktop, twisting through the Anti-Atlas Mountains as evening drained the light from the valleys. Just before nightfall the bus met a pickup truck coming down from Tafraoute. Standing in back were seven, maybe eight, women, dressed all in white, white veils drawn across their faces just under their eyes, otherworldly. When the lights of the bus swept slowly across them their thick headbands of silver coins lit up, one by one, a scatter of starfall pouring from their foreheads, and then we were by them, and night had fallen for good and all.

2.

25 November

"Stupid tourists," he said, looking up from a hand-drawn map of the surrounding country. "They come here, drive around, and think they've seen Tafraoute." I thought he looked something like a tourist himself, but said nothing, following his finger on the map where he was tracing out the best walks. "You must walk here to see anything," he concluded, and with some show of fellow feeling, having decided that I planned on doing some walking myself.

New in town, I imagined any place would be a good place to start, so I set out walking for *Les Rochers Peints* (the Painted Rocks), about eight kilometers by way of the road. And I was happy to be walking in the sun, in the great granite landscape, all rock except for some sandy soil in the flat land along the dry wash next to the road. Because arable land is valuable, most of the houses here have been built among the rocks, or on the rocks, and the close concert of stone landscape and stone and wood houses is peculiarly beautiful. The granite has a pink cast, and most of the houses are pinkish too, running from a light blush to a deep terra cotta. Most of the small villas could be European except for the decoration, the little corbiestep pyramids common at the roof line.

At a turnout I watched a taxiload of tourists happily snapping pictures of the great stone tower that hangs so impressively over Tafraoute. Video cams. No doubt they pitied me my long walk, thinking, "Poor sap, is that any way to spend a vacation?"

After a while, the spring slipped from my step, and I began to trudge. I sensed I was going the wrong way around and realized that if I'd been in a car I could have zipped here and there until I got found. When I crested the hill, as high as the road went, I was dismayed to discover a fork and no sign to tell me which way to the Painted Rocks. Nothing on the road. Nothing, I thought and immediately wondered what that meant. Nothing human here but the road? Something in me, I mused, must think that means nothing here at all. I wandered off down the left fork, then cut over to a flat rock that looked a good place to sit. And it was, the right height and offering an open prospect. I realized, if slowly, that what had drawn me to the rock had drawn many here and for a long time. There were almond shells scattered in a kind of penumbra around the rock, and the lichens on it had a smudged look. When I looked closely, I could make out a web of trails, shaped more or less like a starfish, radiating out from where I sat.

Then I saw a sign in the distance on the fork I hadn't taken and surmised it pointed the way to the Painted Rocks. When I got close enough to read it, I felt found and, walking a little lighter, took the indicated dirt track. The landscape was immense, monumental granite formations on every side, some in spires, some rounded and looking zoomorphic. I got happy and began to wonder what was going to make the Painted Rocks look painted. I noticed that the ground I was walking on was strewn with broken bits of golden silicate, giving the earth itself a glittering, stardust look.

I crossed into a shallow valley and kept on, following the track where it waved over the landscape. Soon I saw a flock of goats coming at me, mostly black but some of them white or pied. Even before I'd seen them, I'd heard the wild calls of the goatherds, two women in dark dresses and veils, running. Across the valley a goat jumped into a tree and began to tear at the foliage.

The landscape that had been so still, every stone feeling placed just so, now surged under the flock. The goatherds pushed them on, running, calling as they came. They were throwing rocks, too, at stubborn goats. When they got closer, I saw they were dressed not in black cotton or wool but in something shimmering, silky, with an embroidered edge, and wearing heavy jewelry. It struck me as odd that in a landscape so monumental, the living—the goats and the goatherds—seemed larger than life, not smaller. Was it the stillness of the landscape that made every motion large?

Then I saw them. The Painted Rocks were just that, painted rocks. I didn't want to believe it; I'd assumed the "paint" was metaphor. It hadn't occurred to me that anything this literal was possible. I walked forward, mouth open. I sat down and then stood back up. No doubt about it, there was something there now!

Most of the rocks I could see at first were painted solid colors—a deep sky blue, a night-sky blue, a gray-cloud color, a few small pink ones to recall the color of the houses down in the valley. Whole rock formations had fallen under the brush. In front of one large, colored conglomeration someone had painted a pseudo-pictograph in green. I walked on, more painted rocks in the distance, maybe a half mile away. Standing stones. A great outcrop in light blue, spangled in pink snakes. I thought it looked like something Christo would have had a hand in and walked on, thinking I'd have preferred the rocks unpainted.

Back in my hotel in town I borrowed a guidebook and discovered the rocks had in fact been painted by Christo in 1982. The scale is certainly grand; I'd never seen anything going under the name of art so big. I couldn't shake those rocks from my mind, but I knew I wanted to. I took heart a little remembering that I'd seen chips of paint everywhere in the sand at the base of the rocks, that already the paint was beginning to go away.

3.

26 November

Dinner at L'Étoile du Sud hadn't been that good. I lingered absently over dessert, almond paste sunk under a golden oil, running my finger through it and licking it off my finger, finding it a little bitter. In the street light outside, just across from my window, a father and a son pushed rental bikes through a shop door into an unlit interior. Watching them, I began to feel wistful—fathers and sons and bicycles, the gleaming spokes spinning, fanning the light out in rays. Tomorrow, I decided, I'd have a ride.

27 November

In full light the bicycles spoke to me but little of nostalgia. I walked around the line of them a couple of times before settling on a purple and green mountain bike bearing the hopeful name Chamois. The grizzled old man working the shop agreed to adjust the seat up. I took a turn. The seat was still low, and I could see the break pads were making only perfunctory contact with the rims. More adjustments, another turn. The seat still wasn't high enough, and the derailer was quirky, refusing the largest sprocket in back. Apparently, at a little less than six feet, I was tall beyond imagining, and I gave up on getting the seat high enough. Just before I rolled out, though, I noticed the tires were low on air. The tire pump at the shop wouldn't do it, and I rode with the son down to an auto repair place in town where they had a pump that worked.

Maybe it was the long buildup, but I felt insanely freed when I pedaled out of town, riding under an arch and on down the blacktop, headed for Taguenza and Tirnmatmat to search out some petroglyphs, gazelles pecked into the local granite. The float of it, the road passing under me like a black river. The boy in me remembered: no hands! For a few minutes I gloried in the smoothness of the motion. Then the narrow little seat began to irritate me, and I noticed that the faster I pedaled, the more I saw of the road, the less of the world I was riding through. The sound of the tires, my own heavy breathing, the rush of air, all together conspired to silence the birds in the trees.

I began to think about getting there, about where I was going. A couple of miles out I noticed that the handlebars seemed bent. I was riding with no hands, just looking, caught in a stupid fascination, when the handlebars began to swivel on their own. For a second I was frightened, expecting the bike to follow their lead and take me for a tumble. But no, I was riding no hands, guiding the bike with my own weight. The handlebars had just worked loose; they weren't possessed, but they were useless now. I drifted to a stop, checked the empty tool pouch and laughed. It wasn't such a long walk back to Tafraoute.

4.

Later, I ate an indifferent lunch, chicken tajine, back at the Star of the South, my adventure on the bike quickly taking the shape of story as I told it to a couple at the next table. It's the way of travelers; narrative is implicit in the going. In the slant sun of afternoon I walked the short, serpentine road up to the Amandiers, an old luxury hotel on the heights. The guidebook I'd borrowed to resolve my questions about the Painted Rocks, the one that had sent me after the gazelles at Taguenza and Tirnmatmat, had mentioned a prehistoric gazelle painted on the rocks at Tazka as well, two kilometers beyond the Amandiers. But the road ends at the hotel and I couldn't see anyway to walk "beyond." So I backtracked, winding down to the blacktop road where it runs into Tafraoute. I approached two happily scuffling schoolboys and asked if they spoke any French. One did. "Ou est la gazelle?" He pointed down a track that joined the road at an acute angle, back where he'd been coming from. I offered him a few dirhams to show me, and off we went. My guide chattered away and then fell silent, his eyebrows arching blackly over almond eyes. Soon we picked up an even smaller boy; if my guide was eight, this boy couldn't have been more than four. The two of them squabbled in Berber. A woman plowed a small field; what she turned over showed wet from the recent rains. Soon Tazka came into view on the left, a few quiet buildings standing among the tumbled boulders of a stone massif. Suddenly, the boys halted and pointed up: petroglyphs, nothing painted here at all.

I handed over the dirhams, giving the smallest boy two or three as well, for tagging along, and the boys ran off. I turned back to the glyphs in silence. They're not gazelles, can't be, but something heavier, more like a mountain goat, with thick horns arched forward over a square-muzzled face. The forms are bigger than life and static, strict profiles pecked into granite. The torsos have been left in natural stone, but the legs, the bounding line around the bodies, and the heads are pecked to an even depth. For petroglyphs, they have a very finished look, halfway to low relief. *La grande gazelle* is worked into the upside of a large granite slab at the base of a cliff. The patina on the worked stone is almost as dark as on the unworked stone; it must be very old or get more of the weather than *la petite gazelle*, pecked into the cliff face above, where the worked stone appears to be a lighter shade of gray. Something of the human here, of the human hand. The glyphs look to the stone from which they are made and toward the cultivated fields immediately below, and on to the village of Tazka. They occupy a space between. I tried to sit with them, in that space, too.

5.

27 November

Late night I dropped into a little restaurant for soup, something thick and yellow, good to dip chunks of black barley bread in. And café au lait. I ate at the coffee bar, as the restaurant proper was given over to men watching soccer on a twelve-inch TV. Every chair was full in there and the overflow standing rapt all around me. At my end of the marble bar I chatted with the barman, who spoke English. I was curious about what the locals think about Christo's Painted Rocks. "Christo?" he asked. "No, no, not Christo," he told me, but a Belgian, Jean Veran, painted those rocks. "A philosopher," he said, "I knew him well." Some guidebook I borrowed, I thought.

Still, I wanted to know how Tafraoutis see those rocks. "For the tourists," he laughed, wiping the counter. "They come from all over to see those rocks. Good for business." He doubted the locals think much about them at all; they're indifferent. Maybe some find them ugly, but he registered no outrage. I told him I had come to Tafraoute to see the unpainted rocks, that a friend's father had said if I liked rocks this was the place, and that my friend had insisted I loved rocks. I didn't try to explain how this had moved me. I didn't understand myself but had made the journey.

When I asked him about getting a bus down the Ameln Valley, he told me it left in the dark, before dawn. His eyes shone, with pride I think, when he understood I meant to walk back, was willing to walk so far to have a good look at the place he called home.

6.

29 November

The blacktop narrowed down until the bus couldn't keep all its tires on the road at once, and the ride got bumpy. Every so often someone rapped on a window with a knuckle or a ring; the driver pulled to a stop, and whoever it was who had done the rapping stepped down. I couldn't tell where we'd got to and was getting edgy, since I would be walking back to Tafraoute and it had begun to seem far.

When I saw a sign for Taguenza, I rapped and stood up, brushed by hooded figures slumped in their seats to the rear door, and jumped. Someone else tossed out a bundle and jumped down behind me. He shouldered his load, not speaking, and trudged after the bus toward the dark village, Taguenza. I looked for a goat trail and, finding one, started up, my breath very white in the dark air. Fifteen minutes of picking my way around small plots of barley plowed into rocks and sand, and I walked into the sun. I turned to it, to accept the day, to be warmed, and to know I was being warmed.

When I found a sitting stone, pink granite, a foot high and not too knobby, I sat down for breakfast. Here too, I noticed, there were weathered almond shells and date pits scattered around the rock. What called me to this particular stone had called to farmers and goatherds before me. The round barley loaves I'd bought in the darkness in Tafraoute were still warm in my day-pack, and I tore off a chunk and began to chew, the quiet of the place coming to me once I was still. I felt around in the bottom of the pack until I found a round of soft cheese and an apple. Slowly, I ate, spreading the cheese on the warm bread, having a bite of apple. I sat, sun-dazzled, the air warming around me, breakfast. Satisfied, I got up, turned my head from the sun to the hillsides glittering behind me, picking one path from among the many that goats had been making there for centuries.

7.

Walking, I thought of the brothers Cain and Abel. One tilled the earth; the other followed the flocks. That was a long time ago, the two boys alone in a green world with their parents. Probably they were good boys, something like the dark-haired children in Tafraoute, the ones with excited eyes. There are still farmers here and those who keep flocks; I've seen them, not doing it much differently from Cain and Abel in their time—the farmer walking behind his one mule, an eye to the plowshare, the goatherd trailing a peeled stick as he walks, crying out to his goats or little dog.

I watched my feet; it was steep and rocky ground. Still, the farmer had been here before me, turning the earth yet again. The earth dies under his plow; all that's left now is a little sand and the weathered stones. I saw where the goats had been, the dry-land grasses chewed back to the ground, the bushes shorn of living green. Goats in trees. I love the beauty of this place, the austerity of sun on shining stone, the clean lines of a land picked to the bone, but this beauty is the work of Cain and Abel. There must be something wrong with the biblical story, where we're led to believe that Cain killed Abel when God found Abel's sacrifice of lambs more pleasing than Cain's sacrifice of the earth's first fruits. The crime, it's said, was fratricide. But I doubt this, for clearly Cain and Abel conspired together to kill the mother, Eve, and have been working together to finish her off ever since. On these slopes in Morocco the deed is as good as done.

8.

The village of Ait Taleb hunched under the rough hills, just above the palm groves that gave it life and that it gave life. I wanted to walk there, but I saw there was a dry gully to be negotiated before I could get to the track that led through the palmery. I descended out of the sun, again walking in cool gloom. I heard children's voices coming from across the valley, soft and clear, and felt lonely for the first time on my long journey. My attention must have lapsed; somehow two wood gatherers had gotten by me without my even realizing they were there: two old women dressed all in black, one with a wicker basket strapped to her back, the ragged ends of firewood spiked over her head like a crown of thorns. The other woman walked under an enormous tangle of brush. She looked like a large shrub in motion. I was startled by their sudden appearance and by their sudden disappearance too, for soon enough only the occasional sound of a turned stone kept me in faith that they were there at all, walking fast in the thick light in the direction of Taguenza. If they had seen me, and they must have seen me, they had given no sign.

Sun in the trees, oak and olives near the road, and the palm groves stretching away wherever there is water. I found it hard to shake the feeling that I was walking in a dream; maybe it was the contrast, as big as between waking and sleeping, of coming off the eroded slopes of the surrounding hillsides into gardens as carefully managed as any I have ever seen. Here, the shape of the earth was made, irregular but patterned terraces watered by a web of small irrigation canals. Under the palms, plots of black earth were planted and showing green—barley and mint, table greens. The deep silence was made deeper by the just audible throb of water in the ditches. No voices, no dishes clinking in the houses that loomed immediately above the worked earth. No sign of people anywhere. I felt as if I was "walking in their sleep."

The track narrowed down to a trail, and I began to doubt how far it would take me. I bent over a stream running in a prepared bed, never a riffle, the surface a pulsing sheen. I watched fish rising to midges under a hand-lettered sign, "La Source," painted over an arrow pointing upstream. Such a sign promises so much to lost souls, but I felt sure it would be just a spring running into a tank somewhere below where the rocks started. I did not go to see.

I came upon the quick at last: a man harvesting dates with a long knife, three women in embroidered black clearing a plot, loading a donkey, avoiding my glance. More women. Many of them faded away before I got close. I didn't feel so much unwelcome as invisible, a ghost walking unseen among the living. But I was not unseen. The pattern of disappearances at my approach, so slow, so casual, was far too regular to be chance. When I did get close, arriving unnoticed in their midst, the women pulled their veils across their eyes with deft hands, and I began to feel how potent a thing a glance can be, how we've worn it down in our lives, let it erode. Just now and again a glance in my world startles, insists on the life that is there.

When I finally walked out of the palmery into the shattered landscape of the valley floor, I felt relieved. A winding trail, looking bleached and worn, ran through the broken fields and on across to a paved road. I got on it and walked, glad to be able to see where I was going. I felt relieved again when I got to the blacktop, relieved to be walking on what I was sure was public property. In the palmeries, I hadn't known, and not knowing, had felt uneasy, an interloper. On pavement, I lengthened out my stride, no longer needing to watch where I put my feet.

Even in winter the sky was a daunting blue. I walked under it. Sometimes a car went by, visible for a long time coming and then going. In a red village I bought a big bottle of Coke and carried it away, feeling small in the landscape. Near the top of a rise I picked my way up a road-cut to sit in the shade of a tree on a rough-hewn stone cube someone had whitewashed a long time ago. *Un rocher peint*, I thought grimly. I sat. The hum of my blood quieted down. From over the rise I began to hear voices. Women's voices, I thought, singing, shreds of conversation, high and easy laughter, that beautiful music. Three women cleared the rise and started down toward me. They were young and dark, walking home probably, maybe from a job in Tafraoute. They seemed to be telling secrets, confidences; they did not see me even when they passed just below where I was sitting on my painted rock. I thought of a phrase from Dante's *La Vita Nuova*, "when the women laugh alone," wondering why it had always seemed so mysterious to me, to speak to me with almost unbearable poignancy of worlds right around me that I can never know. A grasshopper sunned himself on a small stone next to mine. Two of us, one in shadow, one in the sun. He looked old, probably left over from the summer before rather than the first to crawl toward the coming spring.

9.

It's a long incline, and I'd been walking up it for a long time. Over my shoulder I watched a boy on a bike pumping up the hill after me, steady, as if it was something he did often. After a while he came alongside, rode quietly beside me, looking at me out of curious eyes. I tried to explain how I had come to be walking up a hill in his neighborhood. He understood enough to smile in welcome. I fished out a chocolate bar and offered him half, eating the other half myself. We went on, side by side, lost in chocolate. Such a clear face, free of all suspicion. When we got near the crest of the hill, the road got less steep, and my companion said thanks and good-bye and pedaled away, getting smaller on the roadway in front of me.

I stopped to rest. I thought about kinds of motion and about emotion, another kind. However I get around, if my heart remains still, there is no reason for traveling. I looked at the rocky hills: everything there or nothing. Everything, I sang out, *yes*! I began to get angry at the champions of knowledge, those great dismissers. Knowledge, I've got some, and sometimes it helps me to beauty. But I know that recognizing beauty is a small thing; for it to matter, to move me, I'll have to set knowledge aside and simply love. And you can't love with a knowing look on your face.

10.

Talked to a couple from France over breakfast, a round man and a rather pinched woman. They'd been touring Morocco by car, in a white Renault 4. I'd seen a lot of these little cars around, thought them maybe cramped but well suited to the narrow and twisted roads I'd walked on or seen from bus windows. The pair had gotten in late the night before and were driving on to the coast, to beaches that promised to be warm enough to swim. There was a sweep in the way they looked at things, at Morocco, a reach. Today the mountains, tomorrow the sea, a world streaming over the windshield. I drank a second café au lait, watching them pack what looked to me to be big bags. Car journeys. I've taken some. I had intended to rent a Renault myself, to get a feel for how this place would come to me in a car, but sitting there, I decided against it. I know what a car is like, the way speed muffles the world, the way the world rushes at you and then drops forever further into the distance in the rearview mirror. It's a metaphor—life's journey in a day, your finger pressed on fast-forward. I had no reason to hurry; it seemed to me my life was going fast enough.

In Tafraoute a day passes quietly, a slow movement of shadows. Then night comes, and the stars swim. The moon boat sails. Maybe there will be a starfall. I want to have a heart that's ready for it. Not to move so much but to be moved. Love is a motion of the heart.

Two Step on the Threshing Floor

In a cloister, on an island. I sit down in imagination, sit down bodily enough, in a yellow chair at a white table, but in imagination, nevertheless. Everything infused with what it's not but with what I am. The scream of the swifts as they swing in a mass over the roof tiles, into the blue ceiling, *ceil*, of this closed room, unaccountably open to the sky. Sitting at a table away from the door, by the jasmine, in a cloister, on an island, listening to the swifts and the insects and to these and other words, writing some of them down.

Sylvia is still in bed, upstairs, but I have come down, sat down here, fallen, metaphorically, under the spell of a phrase, *in a cloister, on an island*, and all it remembers of being alone. Closed within a world, isolated, by distance, from it. The inside and the outside of solitude.

We are traveling together, after many months apart. We have come south, the direction of the sun, and found it, found each other again, in the heat of the sun and bodies together. And

Patmos, Saturday

Our days on Patmos split between Skala, the harbor town, and Hora, on the hill. We walk the cobbled incline between them often, a ladder between two worlds: the commercial bustle of Skala and the windswept quiet of the hill town with its cloisters, its monasteries. But there is bustle in Hora, too, around the main square; and the shops of Skala do a trade in icons, do business in something beyond business. Perhaps there is no reason to climb the stone path up, nor to come back down again, but we do.

Monday

We go by boat, caïque, to Psili Ammos, to swim. The little boat slips into the waves, and Skala gets smaller all at once, becomes a white line on the shore our wake points to. Hora holds its own on the heights, the white town crystallized around the dark, fortified monastery of Saint John. It is less the victim of distance, but sometimes we lose sight of it when the boat runs close to the abrupt, desert shore.

Everything is dry or water.

The salt sea shows a peacock blue where it's deep, and it gets deep quickly, but there are rocks in the water, small islands the waves surge around. And sunken islands. These show a bright viridian, as if the stone outcroppings below were something luminous and cold, neon, an unseen tension in the relationship of sea and shore.

Not much for the hot lessons of the sun, I spend the day at Psili Ammos in the deep shade of one of several tamarisks, black islands on the hot glare of this beach. Some of the tamarisks grow within a few feet of the sea, and all of them, here, must have their feet in salt. Off and on, all day long, I consider the metaphors.

Looking out of darkness, I see Sylvie spread thin in the sun on our striped sheet. She is reading, I am writing. Later, we eat in the taverna, our chairs stuck deep in sand, goats wandering in and out among the tables.

Sunday

We walk late, when the heat lets go. We go down narrow and narrower roads, always away, until it's too dark to see. We go on and then back, in the dark, conscious of darkness, feeling our way.

Sunday, we turn off the ridge road and walk down a terraced valley to the sea at Lefkes. Sylvia chatters with the goats and with me, her light feet marking the trail. It's close to full dark when we leave the rough beach and head up the two-track dirt road. I stop under a pole, surprised to see an owl overhead, silhouetted, keeping a sharp eye out. He's turned bodily away but tracks us as we pass. I'm pleased to meet the island owls again. I love the birds' arch owlness, what makes an owl so often seem a portent.

Fifty yards further on, I stop at the sound of a quarrel, owls fighting over a perch on the rocks above. Getting down, I can make them out against the sky, hissing and clicking and beating each other with their soft wings. They are owls; their disputes also are intense.

Sylvia hasn't waited, and I see her indistinctly, something white floating over the track up ahead. Before I can overtake her, I see a fourth owl, like the first, quiet on a pole, portentous, and death to rodents.

Monday

The road to Meloi is down along the harbor, up over a low saddle, and down again to water. Coming and going, I stop on the town side to look down on a threshing floor, a rough circle built into a terrace on the slope below the road. It's old, but the flagstone floor was so carefully pieced that the joints look tight even now, the surface smooth enough, almost, for a dance floor. The earth outside is held back by a single row of standing stones at the rim.

The threshing floor has the hard beauty of old stonework, of millstones and Stone Age tools, of dry-stone walls left to the weather a long time ago. But it's still in use. Fine chaff, a golden powder, lies windblown at the margins and shines in the dust downwind.

Coming and going, I turn to Sylvia, to exclaim, but for all that I am speechless, words to dust and blown away.

Lipsi, Tuesday

The island boat to Lipsi and then four hours walking the roads in thick sun. The landscape is all sun, things giving back the heat that's been given to them. We walk, panting at the sheer dazzle of it: the sea a blue gas flame; the yellow terraces, flames; the trees, green torches. We walk, like the rapt over coals, twin wicks suspended over the road. We meet no one, the place emptied out for us to fill, going out of ourselves.

Patmos/Tuesday night

We sit in deep shade—it's night—in the deeper shade of a thick fig tree. If there's a threshold where darkness begins, we've crossed it. We wanted to. We talk, in dusky voices, of Lipsi, of a rough stone cottage where shore meets sea, of a courtyard so small it barely held its one tree, of an island small enough to walk around. Of the threshing floors—one abandoned, one where the threshing had been done, and one surrounded by a golden surf of unthreshed sheaves. We talk about it, how the air over the stone floors seemed to melt and run. We laugh, our laughter not words but still a human sound. We *can* laugh about it; we walked out of that furnace alive.

I imagined, before, that solitude threshes togetherness, but now I think not. Solitude threshes solitude; togetherness, togetherness. We are threshed, thrashed, together or apart, whatever we do.

Troglodyte Nights: In Cappadocia

Getting There

Our taxi felt close to airborne as we rocketed over a rise and dropped down into the Ihlara River valley. Off to the left, the first of the strange sculpted land forms of Cappadocia swept into view, and we began to feel a little arrived.

Our driver ceremoniously pulled a heavy seat belt across his chest, explaining to Sylvia in broken German that since it was Sunday there would be a lot of drunks on the road driving too fast. Out of politeness, he twisted around in his seat to explain, to face us; and as his German was rusty, the explanation took a long time. I watched the road for him, wishing wistfully that he'd gesture less, put his arms down to his sides. "Sonntag," he shouted again, turning back to the road.

Sunday. We'd been hard to convince, but it was true: no buses run from Aksaray to Ihlara on Sundays; finally, we'd conceded the point and hired the taxi. To recover the money I directed the driver to the no-star Star Hotel, a four-dollar-a-head dive on the dusty town square. Our room had three hard beds, more or less the size and shape of coffins, and we lay on them through the heat of the afternoon, in a Sunday funk, considering.

As evening settled in, hunger overcame our prolonged bout of thoughtfulness, and we decided to walk up and out of the valley for dinner at the Anatolia, where we would have stayed if it hadn't been for the expense of the taxi. Our walk up coincided with the cows coming down, a herd of them, in a variety of colors, but if their faces were true, all melancholiacs. A cowherd with a stick trailed behind.

The cobbles seem mortared with gold, but on inspection it proved only the green of the fields alchemized by the strolling cows, who gave good evidence as they passed by. Many of the rough stone houses that lined the road were decorated with pie-sized cow pats, stuck there to dry, I imagined, for burning in winter.

We enjoyed a surprising celebrity with the local children, who shouted "hello" or "merhaba" at the very sight of us. Bright faces. A few rushed up to stick out truly dirty hands for a shake. Hard not to, even if we wondered darkly after who had fashioned the cow droppings into neat pats. One little girl, no more than two or three, ran a hundred-yard dash to us, a smile almost too wide for human, just to shake our hands. We hadn't expected such a welcome, didn't think we were so far off the tourist track, and weren't, we realized, when we heard among the chorus of hellos the occasional dark mutter, "money."

Wading In

Monday, Ihlara

The next morning we strapped on our sandals to hike in the Ihlara Gorge. We'd come to see the green snake of the river where it slides between the red cliffs and to see the churches hewn directly from the cliffs by monks when the place was still called the Peristrema, a long time ago, in the first push of Christian monasticism into Anatolia. The cliffs were willing, a soft tuff—a compressed volcanic ash—that quickly took the shape the monks' simple tools gave it.

When we asked for the trail, an old guy in black drop-seat pants pointed to the cobbled path that ran right above our hotel and then swung his arm in an arc to indicate that the trail was somehow off that way. Wondering how hard can it be, we waved our thanks and set off. We hadn't gotten far, to the first fork, when a boy, a smudged eleven- or twelve-year-old, jumped up to introduce himself, Mustapha. We asked which way to the trail, as best we could, and he pointed down a switchback path to the river. We thanked him and started down, but he was already ahead of us, holding out a hand to help us over any rough going. Oh well, I thought wearily, resigned to paying for the directions later.

The rough bits started pretty quickly, and soon enough we were scrambling like fat lizards on sheer walls over the river and leaping boulder to boulder in the middle of the stream. And then Mustapha rolled his pants up to his knees and waded in, beckoning us to follow. The thought: this can't be right, which I'd been trying to suppress, pressed in. I quizzed Mustapha. Was he sure this was the right trail? He nodded gravely, gesturing downstream.

We looked at the water, at the trailing brown streamers of al-gae, smelled the water, wondered about the sewage system in Il-hara village, looked back over our shoulders to where we'd come from, and decided the trail couldn't be any harder forward than back. We tightened the straps on our sport sandals, Sylvia hiked up her skirt, and we waded in. Mustapha took a sudden interest in Sylvia's safety, holding her arm as she sloshed over the murky bottom. He cooed, she told me later, holding her arm against his chest, whispering something soft and woeful. We were in and out of the river several times. On a last leap, from slippery stone to slippery stone, Sylvia barked her knee good and came up swearing. We were getting near the end of our collective rope, I figured. Then we broke out of the rough into a melon patch; the gorge widened out, and I could see rather clearly the real trail running down an easy incline on the side hill overhead.

I turned to Mustapha, who had his hand out. I put some money in it, saying nothing, not wanting to see him any more. I was sure he'd be hard to shake if I gave him what he deserved.

After a spit bath in our bottled water, we began to walk, trying to put Mustapha behind us. I'd been conned before, expect it where there's poverty and too many people, especially kids. One kid with a racket—but in the same town hadn't another kid, a girl, presented Sylvia a bouquet of wildflowers, only to run off giggling? And then the place rescued us from our thoughts. We walked by garden plots that would have been worked in Byzantine times, and more and more often we saw doorways and windows cut in the rock cliffs. Yellow signs pointed off the main track to small frescoed churches, marked only by a door and occasionally a low-relief facade.

We began to imagine. Here the monks had slept and prayed in the earth, had not built but carved a place for themselves in the world. It wasn't hard to see them, emerging into the light, squinting, or to hear how their chants would have echoed in the valley. For a moment, I saw the monks again, on an Easter, emerging from a lamp-lit church before dawn, coming forth like Lazarus or Jesus himself from the grave, to a slit of starry sky brightening in the east. It wasn't hard to imagine. I thought such lives were lived in beauty.

We came in time to a yellow sign that said *Yılanlı Kilise* (Church of the Snakes). We climbed up the dusty path and found the gaping door, ducked our heads, and went inside. I pointed my small flashlight up to look at the fresco on the domed ceiling. Sylvia did the same. As the beams of our flashlights swept the old paint, we made out, with a start, bats hanging from Christ Pantocrator. They began to stir and talk among themselves; one dropped into the air to flit around us, disturbed.

Polite, not wanting to bother the bats anymore, we crossed to the wall near the door to examine the paintings the church was named for. They weren't so much frescoes as cartoons of women in hell tormented by snakes. The work was badly damaged, but we could make out blue figures on a pale yellow ground. Rows of anguished women's faces. In the foreground, a three-headed serpent writhes, a poor soul in every mouth. To the right, snakes, many snakes, attack four naked women. One of them, her face contorted in terror, suffers a snake to suckle at each of her withered breasts.

What's startling isn't the crouching Satan or the work of his minions but the angel in white, to the left, watching over it all, in serene approbation of the sufferings of the unforgiven.

Sleeping in Earth

Tuesday, Göreme

We arrived in Göreme in a hurry, guts churning. Feeling inclined to snap decisions, we took the first room on offer, at the Sakşagan Otel. "Facilities in the room," which seemed, at the time, for the best. The room itself was simple: the door on one wall, a narrow bed under a bank of windows on the wall facing the courtyard, a blind wall with a second bed, and the bathroom at the back.

It looked a room much like any other, but it wasn't. Like the rock churches of the Peristrema and so much else in Cappadocia, our room was hewn directly from stone, from a pale tuff cone. Many of the *pansiyons* in Göreme have a few "cave rooms" so that travelers there to see the region's cave dwellings can spend troglodyte nights come day's end. If the idea had been to sell the exotic, the execution of that idea had obliterated the very thing the hotel keepers meant to sell—all the difference was on the outside. We peeked into the bathroom at the toilet and the showerhead protruding from the wall, for solace.

With careful timing, we were able to take a few short walks

around Göreme in the afternoon and evening. The clutter of tourist kitsch in the town center is thick on the ground, but even there the fantastic landforms of the place dominate. Rock spires tower over the town buildings in what must be the most phallic landscape anywhere. It's only a matter of time, surely, until Christo or someone else turns up in town with outsize condoms and a crew carrying ladders.

Prudently, we put off the long walks and returned to our cave early. Sylvia showered, and we saw immediately that our troglodyte nights would be compromised by the plumbing. A two-inch-deep puddle formed on the bathroom floor, stranding the commode like some sad island. When the waters hadn't receded by morning, we switched to a room on the other side of the courtyard, which was "built" but dry.

Wednesday

In a fit of confidence we walked the road out of town toward Ürgüp, to the Göreme Open Air Museum, in what was left of the morning cool. We found the landforms along the road, some spires and some shaped like tepees, head-shakingly improbable. To a degree extreme even in Cappadocia, the rock itself has here been inhabited. Almost every outcropping shows a window or a door, and some have been riddled with rooms. The rock is striated, the layers showing the volcanic history of the local geology. The colors range from basalt gray, where the tuff is hardest, through purple and mauve to rose, to stone almost white. Erosion made the landscape and the soil too, which is everywhere cultivated around the great stone outcrops in orchards and vineyards, the ground off-white around the trees and vines.

We trudged on toward the Open Air Museum, as excited as our weakened state allowed but with growing trepidation, as one tour bus after another swept by us, every one raising a cloud of pink dust. By the time we passed the camel concession, we were seriously worried. The place was full of yammering tourists, and nothing is harder to ignore. The monastic occupation must have been dense here; over thirty churches lie within the narrow confines of the museum. But I couldn't visualize the life that had been here for the louts from Omaha or Paris, mostly from Paris, shouting and laughing and crowding in.

What I did notice—and perhaps I was prepared to see it by just how unremarkable our hotel room had proved inside—was that the churches in the Open Air Museum often recalled traditional Byzantine churches, taking no account whatever of the radically different problems and opportunities presented by hewing a church from rock rather than building it freestanding. Most obviously, and superficially, solid stone arches had here and there been painted with red joints, to look as if built of stone blocks. Perhaps this is no different from the way drywall counterfeits lath-and-plaster—or the way lath-and-plaster, as I realized only recently, counterfeits a stone wall. But maybe for the monks, returning to the cave, to troglodytic life, felt like a loss of culture, to be resisted, at least, by decoration.

Surely, and more significantly, the shape of the churches was dictated by the symbolic architecture of Byzantine churches, which must have overidden, to a large extent, any impulse to innovation that the new situation called up. The hewn church, like the built church, would have fulfilled its purpose simply by enclosing a highly articulated sacred space. What was outside, rock or air, whether the enclosed space was hewn from the earth or built on it, would hardly have mattered.

For all that, in Cappadocia, human works—the made place—feel extraordinarily at ease with the natural place, and the natural place better, more interesting, for people having been there. It strikes me now that this concord, although something I look for, appeals to an aesthetic that, however deep its roots, would have been quite alien to the people who hollowed out the churches in the Open Air Museum. Maybe a monk in Cappadocia, deeply involved in the symbolic zoning of space, would not even have seen the concord that calls to me but would have reveled in what the brothers had made *against* nature.

Through the long afternoon we tended our sickness, reflecting grimly on the likelihood that sudden urges would become the leitmotif of our travels. Later, we walked the bent streets of Göreme's old town, walked away from downtown to where townscape gives way to landscape, to agriculture and the sheer muscle of bare stone. Beautiful places. Again, as in Ihlara, children clamored around to chatter "hello," to exchange names, and to shake hands. Again, the big welcome.

We walked on. The neighborhood was alive, the cave dwellings in use, some as homes, some to house animals, and some for storage, for grain or hay or as a place to park a cart for a donkey. The spires that rose here and there over the neighborhood had been hollowed out for pigeons, and the birds were going in and out. The alleys pulsed with life, people living as they knew how, as it's done here and has been, and this conferred an integrity on these cave dwellings we hadn't felt at the Open Air Museum.

Finally, we walked out of town altogether, up high enough to see, standing on a chalky road running through vineyards, Göreme down below taking shelter in the valley. We gazed at the natural chimneys and at the minarets. A muezzin started his singing, and we listened.

Sick at the Born

Thursday/Friday, Ürgüp

We flagged down a *dolmuş* to Ürgüp at the edge of town, though we'd been told, several times, that the service didn't exist. *Dolmuşes* run everywhere in Turkey, so we'd reasoned they'd run the short road between Göreme and Ürgüp too. Perhaps, as travelers, we were expected to take a taxi or a tour bus, to pay more. On a dolmuş, you ride cheap but might be expected to share a seat with a chicken or climb over a basket of figs getting in. The name means stuffed, as in *dolma*, stuffed vegetables, and for the obvious reason. We arrived in Ürgüp feeling virtuous, if compressed.

There followed a roundabout and increasingly urgent tour of the recommended *pansiyons* and hotels, which proved, one after another, full. We began to wonder just how disreputable we might be looking after several weeks on the road. Sylvia's gaze, I thought, seemed somehow less appreciative, more appraising, than it had before.

Finally, we found a room at the Born Hotel, a big Ottoman house that had settled dramatically into its foundations. We were welcomed by another Mustapha, a teenager on a summer internship from a hotel school in Kayseri. We were soon calling him Mustapha II, or Good Mustapha, for his kind attentions and inattentions during our stay (none more appreciated than his refusal to register anything odd in the long hours we lay abed or in the fevered faces we carried into town when we ventured out).

Before the lamentable "exchange of populations" of Greeks and Turks in 1923, Ürgüp had long been an enclave of Anatolian Greeks, and their influence is still visible in the neoclassical buildings and in the abandoned (or converted) churches. Ürgüp too is a valley town, but the landscape is not so novel as at Göreme. Still, troglodytic dwellings are common in the cliffs and side hills overlooking the town proper, though few people live in them anymore. There are two distinct old towns, one occupied (where the Born is) and another, on around the hill, now abandoned. One evening we went there.

A rough track ran in an arc through the more or less dilapidated buildings. Some of them and the weedy slope they occupied had been recently blackened by a brushfire. We were not, at first, encouraged. But soon we were interested and finding it hard to understand how such houses could have been let go. Like some of the houses on the edges of Göreme, most of the houses here were hybrid, a mix of hewn and built structure. Domestic, their design hadn't been as encumbered by precedent as had the troglodytic Byzantine churches. And yet most of the abandoned houses on that black hillside in Ürgüp bore a clear debt to an ancient domestic design, a house built around a courtyard. Such houses, sharing side walls with their neighbors and presenting a continuous, if sinuous, wall to the street, have been common in Anatolia for a very long time, indeed, since ancient times.

Here the design had been remade to include rooms cut from the tuff side hill on one or sometimes two sides of the courtyard (if the situation allowed). The built structure was neoclassical, especially on the facades. The freestanding rooms enjoyed better light and probably better air, while the hewn rooms would have been cool in summer and warm in winter, a gift in the extreme world of Cappadocia. The courtyards were charged with a beauty only half made. The native stone, smooth and zoomorphic, seemed to grow out of the terraced yard into the side hill itself, and the suave shape of the natural stone felt livelier for the doors and windows opening from it. The line between what was built and what was not had been blurred by building from the local stone or painting the whole white, including the live rock. The way these houses were embedded in nature, and nature in the houses, made these dwellings hum, feel profoundly harmonious and grounded. As if an old tension had been, here at least, given rest.

On Edge

Saturday/Sunday, Avanos

Dolmuş—the second syllable is pronounced "mush," what you are after you've been stuffed into a van with too much of the rest of humanity. But passengers already on board can't have welcomed the sight of us either, climbing on with packs strapped to our backs. Once on, there was no turning around, so if we had to get to the rear seats we backed into them, going "beep, beep, beep," like large trucks, to warn the unwary. Still, we preferred the cheap ticket, sure that to spend more would only insulate us from the place and the people we'd come to meet. It's the first law of travel.

So we lodged ourselves into a corner of a *dolmuş* in Ürgüp and set off again, for Avanos on the Kızılırmak River. We arrived confident, free of sickness at last, and began the climb up from the *dolmuş* stop into the old town to the recommended *pansiyon*, the Kervan. We found it without difficulty, but there was no answer when Sylvia rapped on the door. I pushed it open and stepped into the courtyard, calling out. No one answered. I backed out into the cobbled alley, hailing the house once again. A shutter clattered open on the second floor, and an old woman bundled in a black scarf stuck her head out, glowered down at us, and screamed, "No *pansiyon!*"

Our *Rough Guide* promised there was another place just up the hill, the Hittite. We hoped "just" meant close, because the alley up was steep and we were weak, all stamina drained from our legs. We made it but didn't even bother to knock, as weeds grew deep in the doorway. We'd lost faith in the *Rough Guide* weeks earlier, but consulted it one last time, in a kind of fuddled rote. On up, it said, we'd find the Panorama, and it was there and open. And sad. We acquiesced, glancing at the outhouses in the courtyard with a superior air. The owner waived off my proffered passport; the revolutionary overtones of the gesture we understood only after we noticed the big poster of Che Guevara that he'd plastered on the wall over his desk. "*Not,*" I whispered to Sylvia, "auspicious for housekeeping." Sure enough, when we closed the door to our room, we found it could only be "locked" by twisting down a bent nail in the door frame.

And then, at dinner, we were poisoned again. Our frequent,

fevered trips in the dark to the stinking toilets were an agony, suffered but endured.

I remember little of the two days we stayed in Avanos, and what I do remember has the shimmering quality of mirage or hallucination. A table and two chairs set on a sandbar in the middle of a wide river. A cat twitching its last in the dust. A party of loud Italian tourists, arriving late, their bags strapped to a pair of old donkeys. Two of the men later appeared in the courtyard wearing nothing but T-shirts tucked into thong underwear. I managed a low, derisive wolf whistle.

On Sunday we risked a *dolmuş* to the Zelve monastery complex on the Göreme road. We arrived in the late afternoon, not long before closing time. Woozy, we wouldn't have been able to walk a straight line, so we walked a crooked line in. We found the monks had built in two canyons that ran together near the site entrance. To get from one to the other they would have gone down to the junction and come back up again, the long way, or taken the tunnel cut through the canyon walls between. The monastery must have been home to many monks, judging from the honeycombed walls, but a large natural amphitheater that yawns in one cliff face would have been big enough to shelter the entire community in a sudden shower. Although Zelve has its churches, the site as a whole has a more domestic feel than the Open Air Museum at Göreme. In the refectory a stone table with a six-inch-thick top rises directly from the floor of the hollowed room; forty or more could have sat down there together.

At Zelve, more than anywhere else we wandered, dwellings were fashioned without regard to precedent. I remember best a tuff cone, hollowed out in a series of rooms with stairs up and down between, twisting, a spiral of rooms under a skin of stone. Every room had a wall cut close to the surface of the cone, for windows, light and air. No one had ever built like that—how could they have? Such a place could not be built. The monks must have looked to what the stone allowed and to their own needs and taken what the stone gave.

Walking, room to room, through shafts of afternoon sun and by windows where the light was all reflected, I felt subject to the place, the crookedness of my own walk at home on the twist of the stairs. The monks found beauty in what was given, however little they might have looked for it. They learned to live in the earth, to burrow rather than build. Such radical responsiveness requires deep humility, to see what can be done as you do it. You must feel helpless to begin; you cannot know beforehand how to live.

Bus Out

Monday, to Ankara

We thought we knew, anyhow, the way out of Cappadocia. Coming back from Zelve, we'd dropped off the *dolmuş* at the Avanos *otogar* to check bus schedules and settled on the 8:30 for Ankara.

We were there in the morning, carefully dosed with Lomatil for a day on the bus. But the bus was full. We reasoned that Kayseri to Ankara would be a major route; we'd go first to Kayseri. But that bus was full, too. The clerk at the counter thought we'd be able to pick up a bus for Ankara at Nevşehir, so we bought his ticket there. That bus took us as far as Göreme, where, to our surprise, we were herded onto a stuffed *dolmuş* for the ride on to Nevşehir. We were surprised again when the *dolmuş* service ended in downtown Nevşehir, and we had to hire a taxi to get to the *otogar*. There we found that the buses to Ankara were sold out for hours, so we settled again on Kayseri and waited. On board at last, we soon discovered we were going back to Göreme and then, to our dismay, back to Avanos too, back to the very bus station we'd started from hours earlier. Then on to Kayseri under its snowy mountain and finally the long run into the dark and Ankara.

Fool's Journey

"It is in changing that things find repose"
—Heraclitus

1.

27 September, Paros

Fullish moon over dry hills that, in falling into darkness, have lost all depth, become a bounding line only, between earth and sky. Sound of a mason scraping his tools at the end of day.

We make idiot journeys, or set out anyway with a goal we can't forget is mere pretense. Then we try to make something of them, a story perhaps, and fail. And given a stubborn nature, we try again, and fail, and again; and maybe then the failure, still a failure, begins to be of some interest. I sometimes think, and despair, that such stories are most interesting just when they fail completely to give an account of the journey; and I wonder why journeys are necessary at all, but they are.

✿ ✿ ✿

2.

White room. Babbling of voices from the alley below, where pedestrians wander, restless, moving. Phrases in French or Greek, German or English, I never hear enough to make sense of any of it, just the pulsing of language across tongues. And I like hearing that, hearing in it the very impulse to speak.

I said I wanted to catch a trout, a Lahontan cutthroat. We got out the maps. It was going to be a long journey from French-glen. We plotted a great loop—up out of the Blitzen Valley, south and east over Catlow Rim and down toward Denio in Nevada but digressing at Fields, in Pueblo Valley; driving up into the Trout Creek Mountains, finding a place to catch that trout on Trout Creek, then back to Fields and north, with Steens Mountain towering in the west and the Alvord Desert flat as a plate off east; on up to Burns and back around, heading south between Malheur Lake and Harney Lake, paralleling the Malheur Wildlife Refuge, Steens Mountain in the east now, and back to Frenchglen. Almost three hundred miles, a lot of it dirt. To catch a trout.

Of course, such fishing, such travel, always extends beyond itself, has a foot in metaphor if not in mystery. Sometimes only going will resolve a persistent if obscure question or at least cure the fantasy that there is hope in travel or in fishing (and hope seems to reside most in trout fishing). As a boy, I had dreamed of catching a golden trout and kept a shimmering photograph of one pinned to my wall, but I had never made the trip, never tried to actually hook one. It had seemed beyond hope. And I lived to regret my staying home. Sometimes, I think, one must step a little beyond Concord, even if in arguing I have to admit it makes no sense.

I had known about Lahontan cutthroats for years, about Trout Creek. But I had decided I wanted to hold one only recently, when I read in a Portland newspaper that the Fish and Game Commission had proposed closing Trout Creek to all angling to protect the native Lahontans, which they themselves had sometimes trapped to breed for release in other Oregon waters where the native trout had been overrun by hatchery strains (also "planted" by Fish and Game). Then, on a stopover in Bend on our way to Oregon's outback, I'd stood for a long while gazing into an aquarium of Lahontans at the High Desert Museum. They looked melancholy in there, as all fish in tanks do, but beautiful—their gill covers outrageously red, like a girl wearing too much blush but getting away with it—their tails speckled pell-mell with large black dots. For a trout fisherman, for me anyway, there is always the question of the beauty of the fish.

But the desire to fish Trout Creek involved more than that, involved the creek itself. It is home to a pure strain of native Lahontans because it is an isolated drainage and has been for a very long time. The little stream drops down the Trout Creek Mountains, flowing only a little but always, then runs out into the flat land of Pueblo Valley and sinks into the sands. These are waters that never find the sea. The creek fails to fulfill the promise of running water, to be resolved in a great unity of waters in the end. Yet it's in this water that the Lahontans swim, witnessing a wetter time, when the trout were native everywhere and the waters of Trout Creek were joined to other streams on and on.

3. Actual Fishing

2 October, Mount Kynthos, Delos

From here, the islands float upon the suave waves, Rhenia and the islets nearby. Mykonos, Tinos and Syros not so far, all buoyant—all but sacred Delos where I'm sitting securely on a stone.

Delos feels solid, "unmoving," here at the center of the Cyclades. From the windy summit of Kynthos, I suffer a familiar illusion, that I can see everything, or at least more than I can actually see. The islands look small and comprehensible. Down below, the ruins of ancient Delos lie exposed to the white sun, little shadow. On the map in my hand I see the sacred lake, once watched over by the nine marble lions of Delos from the height of their terrace just beyond. But the lake is dry now, and some of the lions have gone. In the absence of a lake someone has put up a stone wall, to show where the lake edge was when swans swam its waters. Just beyond and south lies the two-chambered harbor: to the left the harbor of commerce, which is busy with yachts and excursion boats from Mykonos; to the right the sacred harbor, properly empty, but silted in to the point that a boat would have to drive its prow into the sand to land there now.

At Fields there was a small plane in the parking lot—someone dropped in for pie or groceries. It must have landed on the highway and taxied in to park with the cars; there weren't many. We drove on, after a while seeing to our left the diminishing line of willows where Trout Creek gave out. Soon the road turned up a thin valley, and the creek ran aboveground, zigzagging between the road and where the hill began on the far side, a flood plain sometimes no wider than thirty yards. The creek ran in high, arid country, sometimes between basalt cliffs, but near it the brush was thick—sage and something thorny. We pulled off the road at a turnout, and I geared up—a baby fly rod I hadn't used in years. I waded through the brush in shorts and sandals, remembering William Carlos Williams's wisdom: "You cannot live and keep free of briars," thinking I must really be living now.

I expected the fish to be willing, but getting close to the water proved difficult. Trout Creek, here anyway, watered the willows first, and they grew thick to show their appreciation. Too thick, most places, to get a line in the water. Where it was open enough, the trout spooked at any motion and in their darting spooked the fish in the next pool, too. Finally, I found a chute where the creek ran only two feet wide over lava blocks, a whitewater rush in heavy shade, where my approach went undetected. I stripped off a little line and shook my hopper down the current. In the first dark pocket there was a slashing take I missed, but when she came back I hooked her: willing, like a wild trout in a small desert stream. I managed to keep her out of the brush; in my hand the Lahontan colors shone from under a silver sheen—the flushed look on the gill covers and the big spots.

I caught another one in a cow pasture a little later, standing midstream and making a long cast up an alley of willows. And I hooked a few others: every one of them took to the air, as if suddenly finding water too thick for living, trying to translate themselves into something more airy, something more like a bird. Most of them escaped me, anyway, in trying.

After a while, Keith and I trailed back to the car, leaving the Lahontans to swim, ignorant, I imagine, how little downstream was available to them. We stopped for a while to watch some chukars climb the rock slide opposite, talking as they went, just as if they'd forgotten how to fly.

4.

4 October, Naxos

A windy morning, clouds streaming across the sun, shadows darkening the island. The wind registers in the talk of those walking the alley below this terrace: les vents, oi anemoi, die Winde, *those winds—what boats will sail today?*

On the town side of things I look down into a walled garden, now mostly finished for the season, but there are still lemons and limes in the trees and pomegranates. Only this morning I noticed

*an odd thing about the garden: the blue, bleached door is pad-
locked by two rusty rings on the outside, but it's also barred from
within.*

Dust devils danced on the floor of Pueblo Valley as we passed
again the end of Trout Creek. On to Fields and the turn north
along the broken edge of the great escarpment that is Steens
Mountain. From the west it is a long, gentle pull up to the summit, but on the east it's a dead drop. Driving, we looked up to it.

We were going north just to avoid going the same way back to
Frenchglen and had settled on a stew in the Alvord Hot Springs
as an excuse for the extra miles. On the map, I noticed, Alvord
Lake appeared as a blue bounding line, the interior crossed by
diagonal blue lines, under the legend "dry." I got out another
map, where it appeared all blue, but again with the notation
"dry." Keith and I laughed a little about our maps, mapping what
wasn't there, the memory of a lake. And there are dry lake beds
everywhere out in Harney and Malheur counties; why are some
on the map, some not? Is it the force of a name? In high-water
years we'd seen water in Alvord Lake, and in other years nothing
there; we had to acknowledge the difficulty. But we'd seen water
in lots of places in the mid-eighties where no lakes showed on either of these maps, seen Harney Lake and Malheur Lake join
right over the highway as well, to form one lake, and yet this
greater lake never got a name of its own before the waters receded.

Sometime after Fields we started seeing water—or mirage—
off near the horizon, a sheer, silky blue. We looked and looked
and argued, unable to decide if something was there or not or if
an illusion was the thing that was there. We were almost by it before we knew for certain that there was a little water at the far
edge of the alkali flats. By then, we were laughing at ourselves.

We crossed over the low rise between Alvord "lake" and the
Alvord Desert and saw immediately that there was a lot more

water in the desert than there had been in the lake. We were surprised but not too surprised, because we'd seen water in the desert another time, from high up on the broken edge of Steens Mountain. That day we'd heard that the location of the lake in the desert shifted day by day, even hour by hour, depending on the quarter of the wind. The Alvord is that flat, and on it the "lake" had wandered. Although it looked like a lake, it was almost without depth, so if you imagined a lake there, it verged on illusion.

5. Into the Caldera

7 October, Santorini

To arrive at Santorini by water is to float into the throat of the volcano, into the caldera, lava cliffs all around. There was a mountain, and arriving ships sail into its absence; where there was a mountain, now there is none, just a rim of island to remember where its slopes once climbed to a summit. It has been gone for 3,500 years, but its memory hangs yet in the sky over the caldera or in the mind's eye. The volcano that created the mountain and then did the damage is still live. On the black lava islet of Nea Kameni, in the center of the bay, the smell of sulfur rises yet from the hot springs bubbling up from underground.

I arrived yesterday, drifted to port on a ferry, weary. Today my table is set by a window swung out over the caldera, set, like the little town of Fira, directly on the cliff edge as if on a dare or as a mad assertion of how we must live. The damage has been done, nothing doing but to build regardless on what remains.

I sit at this table and grip my pen, telling myself, hang on.

Keith slowed the car when the cement tanks at Alvord Hot Springs showed at last on the right. We were surprised to see

somebody down there but decided to have a look and maybe a
soak anyway. The path from the highway down to the bathing
tanks parallels the water from the springs that runs too hot to
touch and smelling eggy. It makes a little stream, which meanders steaming through ground crusted white with mineral de-
posits and choked with orange and green slime. So I wasn't too
disappointed to discover that three lean ranchers had emptied
the tanks for a once-a-year cleaning—no bathing that day. They
were coots, and we liked them, but what we were they weren't
too sure. Finally, in a tribute to what two weeks in the desert can
do to a man, one of the ranchers asked, "Is you fellas sheep
herders or somethin'?"

We drove on, but it was as ghosts of travelers; we journeyed
beyond what we knew to be the end of the story—just to get
back to Frenchglen. It often turns out this way. And traveling
beyond the end of the story, where sometimes meaning is made
or sustained, always raises the rancher's question about who we
are. Traveling far enough, maybe, the question becomes not
who but what.

ACKNOWLEDGMENTS

I am grateful to the Eberly College of Arts & Sciences of West Virginia University for a sabbatical leave and to the Fulbright Commission for six months in Greece. Without their support, much of this book would not have been written.

Finally, I am indebted to my fellow travelers, who have taught me so much of what I know about being here: Keith Oderman, CEO, Tom and Nick Condon, Sylvia Torning, Jeff Mann, Parveen Seehra, David Miller, Winston Fuller and Louise Lamar-Fuller, Tom Miles, Diana Abu-Jaber, David James Duncan, John Bussanich, James Harms, Tim and Gail Adams, Bonnie Anderson, Rip Cohen, James Houlihan, and Nick Tingle; among the Greeks, Vasiliki Xatzi, Avra Sidiropoulou, Anastasia Theodorou, and Fereniki Kapetaniou. And, at last, Sara Pritchard.

ABOUT THE AUTHOR

Kevin Oderman is Professor of English at West Virginia University, where he teaches American literature and creative writing. Over the last ten years, his essays have appeared in the *Northwest Review*, *Southwest Review*, *North American Review*, in *Shenandoah*, and in several other literary journals. He has twice taught abroad on Fulbrights, first in Thessaloniki, Greece, and subsequently in Lahore, Pakistan.